Colin F. Taylor, Ph. D.

Sitting Bull
and the White Man's Religion

Colin F. Taylor, Ph. D.

Sitting Bull
and the White Man's Religion

Sitting Bull und die Religion des weißen Mannes

Early missionaries in North America

Frühe Missionare in Nordamerika

Verlag für Amerikanistik
Wyk auf Foehr
Germany

Enhanced and revised version of a paper given at the University of Lund, Sweden, to the 20th American Indian Workshop "Native American Religions", April 26-28 1999.

Erweiterte und überarbeitete Fassung eines Vortrags vom 20. American Indian Workshop zu dem Thema "Native American Religions", 26. - 28. April 1999, Universität Lund, Schweden.

Images/Abbildungen: **Colin F. Taylor**

Übersetzung aus dem Englischen: Helga und Dietmar Kuegler

ISBN 3-89510-100-1

1. Auflage 2000

"Tatanka Press" Vol. 1

Copyright © 2000 by "Tatanka Press", an Imprint of VERLAG FÜR AMERI-KANISTIK D. KUEGLER, P. O. Box 1332, D-25931 Wyk, Germany

Satzherstellung: Druckerei R. Knust GmbH, 38104 Braunschweig
Druck und Reproarbeiten: Druckerei R. Knust GmbH, 38104 Braunschweig
Buchbinderische Verarbeitung: Industriebuchbinderei Bratherig GmbH, 38118 Braunschweig

Alle Rechte der Verbreitung, in jeglicher Form und Technik, vorbehalten!
Printed in Germany

Contents / Inhalt

Introduction/Einführung	7
Francis la Flesche's protest: the problem of translation	8
Der Protest von Francis la Flesche: Das Übersetzungsproblem	9
The world of Sitting Bull	9
Die Welt Sitting Bulls	10
Plains Indian religious concepts	11
Religiöse Konzepte der Plainsindianer	11
Father De Smet and Sitting Bull	14
Father De Smet und Sitting Bull	14
Sitting Bull's Retreat to Canada in 1877	19
Sitting Bulls Rückzug nach Kanada 1877	19
Prisoners of War	23
Kriegsgefangene	23
A robe for the Pope	25
Eine Robe für den Papst	25
Back home at last!	29
Endlich Daheim!	29
The Ghost Dance and death of Sitting Bull	30
Der Geistertanz und der Tod Sitting Bulls	31
Marker at Grand River	33
Gedenktafel am Grand River	34
Sitting Bull today	34
Sitting Bull heute	36
The Sioux and Catholic Religion today	36
Die Sioux und die katholische Religion heute	37
Acknowledgements	38
Danksagung	40

Appendix I: Sitting Bull or Supreme Bull? 41
Anhang I: Sitting Bull oder Supreme Bull? 41

    Introduction/Einführung 41

    Background to the subject 41
    Hintergrund des Themas 41

    Renderings of Sitting Bull's name 43
    Übertragungen von Sitting Bulls Namen 43

    Sitting Bull prior to circa 1880 44
    Sitting Bull vor 1880 45

    Linguistics of a name 45
    Der Name in der Linguistik 46

Appendix II: A robe for the Pope 50
Anhang II: Eine Robe für den Papst 50

    Introduction/Einführung 50

    Description of the robe 51
    Beschreibung der Robe 51

    Sitting Bull's contact with Catholic missionaries 53
    Sitting Bulls Kontakt mit katholischen Missionaren 53

    Acquisition of a painted robe and transfer to Europe 58
    Der Erwerb einer bemalten Robe und ihr Transfer nach Europa 58

Fußnoten 62
Footnotes 63

Bibliography 70
Bibliographie 70

Captions for cover and frontispiece 76
Bildlegenden für Titelbild und Frontispiz 76

Einführung

Weisse Missionare waren schon früh in Nordamerika aktiv, um den Indianerstämmen das Christentum zu verkünden. Viele der Bekehrten stammten jedoch aus unterworfenen, besiegten Völkern. Sie wurden von den unabhängigeren Gruppen als "Betende Indianer" verspottet. Zweifellos handelte es sich dabei um eine Diskriminierung, da Völker wie die mächtigen Mohegan, die Narraganset und andere die Religion des weissen Mannes strikt ablehnten. Daher ging Mitte des 17. Jh. Metacom (auch "King Philip" genannt), ein bedeutender Wampanoag-Häuptling, soweit, dem Congregationalisten-Missionar John Eliot voller Verachtung zu erklären, dass er sich "so wenig für sein Evangelium interessiere, wie für einen Knopf an seinem Mantel!"[1]

Indianer zum Christentum zu bekehren, war harte Arbeit. Es scheint, dass die nordamerikanischen Indianer grösstenteils zufrieden mit ihren eigenen religiösen Überzeugungen waren. Allerdings ist belegt, dass sie anderen Lehren mit Neugier begegneten, insbesondere der Römisch-Katholischen Kirche, höchst beeindruckt vom zeremoniellen Pomp, der Teil des katholischen Ritus war. Zudem gab es - und viele ihrer Führer erkannten dies im Laufe der Jahrhunderte - zahlreiche praktische

Introduction

White missionaries were early active in North America, for the instruction of tribes in Christianity. Many of the converts, however, were drawn from broken, defeated tribes and were referred to, by more independent groups, as 'Praying Indians'. Undoubtedly, this was a derogatory term, for such tribes as the powerful Mohegan, Narraganset, and others, firmly rejected the white man's religion. Thus, in the mid-1600s, Metacom (referred to as 'King Philip'), an important chief of the Wampanoag, went so far as to scornfully tell the Congregational missionary, John Eliot, that "he cared no more for his gospel than for a button upon his coat"![1]

Converting Indians to Christianity was hard work; North American Indians, it seems, were largely satisfied with their own religious beliefs. There is, however, good evidence that they were curious of others and, particularly in the case of the Roman Catholic religion, much impressed with the pomp and ceremonial which was such a part of Catholic ritual. In addition – and many American leaders over the centuries recognized this – there were several practical advantages with missionary contacts. In particular, the dedication and abilities of the white missionaries, led a number of them to both learn and record the

Vorteile durch den Kontakt mit den Missionaren. Einige weisse Missionare brachten zudem die Hingabe und Fähigkeit auf, die Sprache des jeweiligen Stammes, mit dem sie in Kontakt kamen, zu lernen und aufzuzeichnen. Diese Sprache konnte dann aufgeschrieben werden - etwa mit einer Mischung aus Piktographien und Zeichen, die Le Clerq benutzte -, um das Vaterunser in Micmac für die Stämme von Cape Breton und Nova Scotia niederzuschreiben.

Mit der Verlagerung der Missionsarbeit nach Westen weiteten sich diese Tätigkeiten aus. Beispielsweise unterrichteten 1835 Dr. Thomas Williamson und Stephen Riggs unter der Schirmherrschaft des "American Board of Commissioners for Foreign Missions" (ABCFM) Santee und Mdewakanton Sioux im Lesen und Schreiben der Dakota-Sprache. Etwa eine Generation später erkannten sogar so überzeugte und patriotische Führer wie Sitting Bull die Bedeutung der Gabe des weissen Mannes durch die Missionare und forderten die Lakota-Kinder auf, sich diese Fähigkeiten anzueignen - obwohl er sie zugleich ermahnte, Indianer zu bleiben und die Werte der religiösen Überzeugungen ihrer Stämme unterstrich.[2]

language of the tribe with whom they came into contact. That language could then be written – such as the blend of pictographs and glyphs used by Le Clercq to record the Lord's Prayer in Micmac for the tribes of Cape Breton and Nova Scotia. These activities were extended with the western expansion of missionary work. By 1835, for example, Dr. Thomas Williamson and Stephen Riggs, under the auspices of the American Board of Commissioners for Foreign Missions (ABCFM), were instructing Santee and Mdewakanton Sioux, to read and write Dakota.

A generation or so later, even such fiercely patriotic leaders as Sitting Bull, recognized the importance of this white man's gift from the missionary workers and urged Lakota children to acquire the skills – although he cautioned them to remain Indians and emphasized the value of tribal religious beliefs.[2]

Francis la Flesche's protest: the problem of translation

If, for several reasons, Indians were curious about the white man's religion, there is very little to indicate that the reverse was true. Francis la Flesche, a much respected Omaha scholar, summed up a somewhat

Der Protest von Francis La Flesche: Das Übersetzungsproblem

Wenn auch Indianer aus verschiedenen Gründen an der Religion des weissen Mannes Interesse zeigten, so gibt es nur wenige Belege, dass dies auch umgekehrt der Fall war. Francis La Flesche, ein hochangesehener Omaha-Wissenschaftler, beschrieb eine recht weit verbreitete Ansicht, als er feststellte, dass die Missionare im allgemeinen die Überzeugung vertraten, dass "allein die weisse Rasse ... im Besitz des Wissens über einen Gott" war. Somit wurden die Mythen, Rituale und Legenden der amerikanischen Indianer häufig in einer Weise dokumentiert, die ihre wahre Bedeutung verzerrte und sie "kindisch oder närrisch" erscheinen liess.

La Flesche hob die Unterschiede im Vorstellungsvermögen und in der Weltsicht hervor und wies darauf hin, dass Geist und Form der indianischen Denkweise oft in der wörtlichen Übersetzung durch Wissenschaftler verloren ging. Mehr noch: Diese unzulänglichen Übersetzungen wurden zur Beurteilung der geistigen Fähigkeiten der Indianer herangezogen und um Erkenntnisse über deren Konzepte von einer höheren Wesenheit zu gewinnen.[3] Es waren diese Einstellungen, mit denen der hochangesehene Hunk-

widespread attitude when he recorded that missionaries generally entertained the idea that the 'white race ... alone possess the knowledge of a God' and that the myths, rituals and legends of the American Indian were frequently recorded in such a manner as to obscure their true meaning and made them appear as 'childish or as foolish'. La Flesche noted the differences in imagery and world views and that both spirit and form of American Indian thinking were often lost in the literal translation by scholars. Further, these limited translations were then invariably used to judge the mental capacity of the Indian and to draw conclusions about his conception of a Supreme Being.[3]

It was such attitudes which confronted the much respected Hunkpapa Sioux leader, T'at'aŋ'ka 'Iyótaŋke – known to the world as Sitting Bull – when he first made contact with white missionaries in the 1860s.

The World of Sitting Bull

Sitting Bull was born in March 1831 at a place called Many-Caches on the Grand River in present-day South Dakota. His father was the distinguished warrior, Returns Again, and his mother, Her Holy Door. At an early age, he displayed

papa Sioux Führer *T'at'aŋ'ka 'Iyótaŋke* - der Welt als "Sitting Bull" bekannt - konfrontiert wurde, als er in den 1860er Jahren die ersten Kontakte zu weissen Missionaren knüpfte.

Die Welt Sitting Bulls

Sitting Bull wurde im März 1831 an einem Ort namens Many-Caches am Grand River im heutigen South Dakota geboren. Sein Vater war der angesehene Krieger Returns Again, seine Mutter war Her-Holy-Door. Schon sehr früh zeigte er ungewöhnliche Eigenschaften. Er verhielt sich stets sehr umsichtig. Er bedachte die Dinge äusserst sorgfältig, bevor er handelte, und stets analysierte er die Handlungen und Äusserungen anderer, bevor er reagierte. Daher erhielt er als Kind den Spitznamen *"Hunkeshnee"* oder, wie von einem Sioux-Informanten 1964 in Fort Yates ins Englische übersetzt, "Thoughtful One" (Der Nachdenkliche).[4]
Schon als Junge tat er sich als fähiger Jäger und tapferer Krieger hervor, tötete seinen ersten Bison mit zehn und zählte den ersten Coup an einem feindlichen Crow im Alter von fünfzehn. Es war zu dieser Zeit, als sein Vater ihm den Namen *T'at'aŋka I'yotake* verlieh, der ihm durch eine mystische und merk-

unusual traits, always acting in a very deliberate fashion, thinking things over very carefully before taking any actions and he always analysed others' actions and words before responding: thus, his childhood nickname became *Hunkeshnee* or, as rendered by a Sioux informant at Fort Yates in 1964, 'Thoughtful [One]' in the English language.[4]
At an early age, he distinguished himself as a skilled hunter and brave warrior, killing his first buffalo at the age of ten and counting his first coup on a Crow antagonist at the age of fifteen. It was then, his father bestowed on him the name *T'at'aŋka I'yotake* a name which was received by his father from mystical and strange encounter with a lone buffalo bull. The *wakan* experience, caused Returns Again and his three companions, to be awestruck; the buffalo, it was later reported, left four names with Returns Again – Sitting Bull, Jumping Bull, Bull Standing with Cow and Lone Bull. It was his privilege, it was explained, to use and bestow these names as he saw fit. The names too represented the four ages of life: Infancy, Youth, Maturity and Old Age.[5]

würdige Begegnung mit einem einsamen Bisonbullen übermittelt wurde. Returns Again und seine drei Begleiter waren nach dieser *Wakan*-Erfahrung von Ehrfurcht ergriffen. Der Bison, so wurde später berichtet, überliess Returns Again vier Namen - Sitting Bull, Jumping Bull, Bull Standing with Cow und Lone Bull. Er erhielt angeblich das Privileg, diese Namen so verleihen, wie es ihm angemessen erschien. Die Namen repräsentierten ausserdem die vier Abschnitte des Lebens: Kindheit, Jugend, Reife und Alter.[5]

Religiöse Konzepte der Plainsindianer

Die Plainsindianer hatten eine komplexe Vorstellung von höheren Mächten, die allerdings - wie in allen Kulturen - nur von einer begrenzten Zahl Menschen verstanden wurde. Die grundlegenden religiösen Konzepte bezogen sich auf ein Universum, das aus drei parallelen Welten bestand: Unterwassergeister des Sees, in dem die Erde schwamm, Geister, die den Lebensraum der Tiere und Pflanzen an Land und im Wasser beherrschten, und jenseits der blauen Himmelskuppel lag das Reich der Oberwelt, das von Geistern regiert wurde, die ihre Entsprechung in der

Plains Indian Religious Concepts

The Plains Indian view of the higher powers was complex and, as in all societies, only understood by a limited number of individuals. Basic religious concepts referred to a universe consisting of three parallel worlds. Underwater spirits in the lake on which the Earth floated; spirits whose domain included animals and plants on land and in the water; and beyond the dome of the blue sky, lay the realm of the upper world, dominated by spirits matching those of the underworld, the most powerful of which were the Thunderbirds.

Individuals versed in the religious concepts of their people, however, identified a more complex pattern than this. Thus, for example, in the case of the Cheyenne, the religious concepts and cosmology were divided into more layers into which Cheyenne story, ritual and religious symbolism could be fitted. Whilst fundamentally not much different from the Christian idea of heaven, earth and hell (although some may disagree), on several counts the patterns are actually more sophisticated and complex.[6] Thus, Dr. J. R. Walker, after years of research, finally identified the Lakota *Tobtob kin*, or four times four. Here, we have a hierarchy of spirits who were

Unterwelt hatten. Die mächtigsten unter ihnen waren die Donnervögel. Personen, die in den religiösen Konzepten ihrer Völker kundig waren, klassifizierten jedoch ein umfangreicheres Muster als dieses. So waren beispielsweise bei den Cheyenne die religiösen Vorstellungen und die Weltsicht vielfach abgestuft, so dass die Geschichte und der rituelle und religiöse Symbolismus eingeordnet werden konnten. Gab es grundsätzlich auch geringe Unterschiede zu den christlichen Ideen von Himmel, Erde und Hölle - auch wenn manche damit nicht übereinstimmen -, so sind die Denkmuster in vielen Fällen ausgefeilter und komplizierter.[6] Dr. J. R. Walker identifizierte nach jahrelanger Forschung schliesslich das *Tobtob kin*, oder Vier-mal-vier der Lakota. Hier haben wir eine Hierarchie der Geister, die eindeutig mit den oralen religiösen Konzepten der Stammesintellektuellen verbunden und definiert ist.[7] Es gibt nur wenige Belege die die Vermutung zulassen, dass es den Missionaren gelang - oder dass es sie auch nur interessierte -, die komplexen Vorstellungen der Plainsindianerreligion zu begreifen, obwohl mindestens ein angesehener und ausgebildeter Anthropologe, Robert H. Lowie, anerkannte, dass sich Stammesintellektuelle ernsthaft mit den Rätseln des Universums auseinandergesetzt hatten.

clearly linked and defined in the oral religious concepts of the tribal intellectuals.[7] Little evidence exists which suggests that the missionaries themselves managed, or indeed even bothered, to identify these complex ideas of Plains Indian religion, although at least one respected and trained anthropologist, Robert H. Lowie, recognized that tribal intellectuals had indeed grappled with the riddles of the universe. One such 'tribal intellectual', as referred to by Lowie, was unquestionably the Hunkpapa Sioux spiritual leader, Sitting Bull. There was by the Sioux, however, a subtle rendering of his name which seems to have gone largely unrecognized but which reinforces the notion that in buffalo hunting days, he was held in particular esteem by the Sioux and further underlines the observations of Francis La Flesche, of distortion possibly occurring and true meanings being masked, by small but significant errors occurring in translation. Certainly in his later years, Sitting Bull was actually referred to by the Lakota as *T'at'ŋ'ka 'Iyótaŋke* **not** *T'at'aŋ'ka 'I'yotake*.[8] The former perhaps best translates to 'Supreme Bull' and the latter to 'Sitting Bull'. 'Supreme Bull' comes close to expressing the very high regard with which Indian people held this man and which was reported on by Dr. Thomas B.

Ein solcher "Stammesintellektueller", wie Lowie ihn nennt, war fraglos der spirituelle Hunkpapa-Sioux-Führer Sitting Bull. Es gab bei den Sioux eine subtile Auslegung seines Namens, die offenbar grösstenteils unberücksichtigt blieb, die aber im Hinblick darauf, dass er in den Tagen der Bisonjagd in besonderer Achtung bei den Sioux stand, die Beobachtung von Francis La Flesche, dass Erscheinung und wahre Bedeutung durch kleine aber bedeutsame Fehler in der Übersetzung verschleiert wurden, unterstreicht. In späteren Jahren wurde Sitting Bull von den Lakota mit Sicherheit tatsächlich *T'at'η'ka 'Iyótaηke* **nicht** *T'at'aη'ka 'T'yotake genannt.*[8] Ersterer Name wird vielleicht am genauesten als "Der höchste Büffel" übersetzt, der zweite als "Sitzender Büffel". "Supreme Bull" entspricht sehr genau dem hohen Ansehen, das dieser Mann unter Indianern genoss. Dr. Thomas B. Marquis berichtete Anfang dieses Jahrhunderts darüber. Marquis erklärte, dass der männliche Bison von allen Plainsindianern verehrt und dem "omnipräsenten Geist am nächsten angesehen wurde, da er das weiseste und stärkste unter allen Tieren war". Ein Mann, der "nach dem Bisonbullen benannt wurde, nahm den höchsten Status unter seinen Mitmenschen ein" (Marquis 1934: 8). Der Name weist

Marquis in the early years of this century. Marquis pointed out that the buffalo bull was honoured by all Plains Indians and was considered 'closest to the Everywhere Spirit, as being the most wise, as well as the most powerful, of all animals'. A man so named 'for the buffalo bull was rated as having that highest status among his human companions' (Marquis, 1934:8). The name makes reference to a great provider, one who is generous, forthright, kind and considerate – especially to children and the old. (A full discussion of Sitting Bull's "real" name is in Appendix I.)

ihn als grossen Versorger aus, einen der grosszügig, ehrlich, freundlich und rücksichtsvoll ist - besonders zu Kindern und Alten. (Eine vollständige Erörterung von Sitting Bulls korrektem Namen erfolgt im Anhang.)

Father De Smet und Sitting Bull

Im Juni 1868 traf der Jesuitenpriester Father Pierre-Jean De Smet am Powder River mit den Teton Sioux zusammen (Abb. 1). Hier machte er sich ohne Zweifel die Vorliebe der Plainsindianer für Prunk und Zeremonielles zunutze, als er für die Vorbereitung einer Messe Flaggen hisste und ein Kreuz aufrichtete. Vielleicht regte De Smet die Vorstellungen der Sioux von religiösen Konzepten sogar stärker an als es ihm selbst bewusst war, und es war nicht nur das Bild der Heiligen Jungfrau, die von einem Heiligenschein aus Sternen umgeben wurde, mit dem eine der Fahnen verziert war. Jahre später berichtete Alice Fletcher, dass die Oglala, die sie 1882 besuchte, bei formellen Gebeten im allgemeinen Pfähle mit daran befestigten Stoffbahnen aufrichteten. Sie glaubten, dass das im Wind flatternde Tuch die Aufmerksamkeit der höchst sensiblen Geister erregen würde, die

Father De Smet and Sitting Bull

In June 1868, the Jesuit priest, Father Pierre-Jean De Smet, met up with the Teton Sioux on the Powder River (Fig. 1). Here, without doubt, he appealed to the Plains Indians' love of pomp and ceremony when, in preparation for a sermon, he mounted banners and a cross above the meeting. De Smet may have appealed more to the Sioux' idea of religious concepts than he realized and it was not just the picture of the Blessed Virgin surrounded by a halo of stars which was embellished on the banner. Years later, Alice Fletcher reported that the Oglalas she had visited in 1882, generally raised poles with pendants of calico tied to them when formal prayers were made and that the fluttering of the material was supposed to attract attention and ensure that the appeal was heard, the spirits being thought very sensitive to any artificial disturbance of the atmosphere. In most ceremonies, the person most closely interested was forbidden to shake his garments, move his arms violently, run, or talk loudly, since this would trouble and affect the spirit. Little wonder that, during the Sioux rendezvous with De Smet, the Indians were both attentive and silent and looked with more than idle curiosity at the banner!

Figure 1 Father Pierre-Jean De Smet's conference with the Hunkpapa and Blackfeet Sioux in 1868. Note the Marian banner which he gave the Sioux as a "holy emblem of peace". De Smet lodged with Sitting Bull who he described as the "generalissimo of the warriors". From an early water-colour. Courtesy, De Smetiana Collection, Jesuit Missouri Province Archives, St. Louis.

Abb. 1 Father Pierre-Jean De Smets Konferenz mit den Hunkpapa- und Blackfeet-Sioux 1868. Auffällig die Marienflagge, die er den Sioux als "heiliges Emblem des Friedens" schenkte. De Smet wohnte bei Sitting Bull, den er als "Generalissimus der Krieger" beschrieb. Von einem frühen Aquarell. Mit Genehmigung der De Smetiana Collection, Jesuit Missouri Province Archives, St. Louis.

besonders empfindlich auf künstliche Störungen der Atmosphäre reagierten, so dass die Gebete erhört werden würden. In den meisten Zeremonien war es der am stärksten involvierten Person verboten, ihre Kleidung zu schütteln, die Arme heftig zu bewegen, zu rennen und laut zu sprechen, weil all dies den Geist verärgern und beeinflussen würde. Es war somit nicht verwunderlich, dass die Sioux während des Treffens mit De Smet aufmerksam und still waren und die Fahne mit grosser Neugier beobachteten.

Der christliche Symbolismus ging über Verkündigungen und verzierte Fahnen hinaus. De Smet segnete viele Kinder, taufte eine Anzahl Krieger und gab Sitting Bull ein Kruzifix aus Messing und Holz - eines von mehreren, die er angeblich an einflussreiche Plainsführer verschenkte. Sowohl das griechische als auch das lateinische Kreuz, manchmal mit zwei Querbalken statt mit einem, waren vertraute Symbole für die Sioux. Sie stellten die 4 Winde oder die schwer zu treffende Libelle dar. Kreuze konnten religiöse oder militärische Bedeutung haben. Mit ihnen wurden höhere Mächte beschworen, nicht zuletzt jene, die Schutz boten. Deutlich gesagt: Wenn Missionare bei ihrem Einzug in ein Lager Kreuze vor sich hertrugen, erweckten sie Gefühle,

Christian religious symbolism was advanced several stages beyond preaching and embellished banners, because De Smet blessed many children, baptized a number of warriors and gave a crucifix of brass and wood to Sitting Bull – one of several that he was said to have given to influential Plains leaders. Both the Greek cross and Latin cross, sometimes with two crossbars instead of one, were familiar symbols to the Sioux, representing the four winds or the hard-to-hit dragonfly. The crosses were religious or military symbols used to evoke higher powers, not least those of protection. Clearly, when missionaries carried crosses before them as they marched into encampments, they evoked a number of sentiments already well established amongst the very people they sought to convert. The similarity of motifs is often surprising; the double Lorraine cross embellished on the walls of a Catholic church in France, is mirrored by one painted on a Sioux shield in the Smithsonian Institution collections in Washington. At times, however, the commonality of signs with different symbolic meanings, caused some confusion (see Taylor, 1994 (a):62-63).

Sitting Bull greatly coveted the crucifix given to him by Father De Smet and he is recorded as wearing it on several occasions in subsequent

die gerade unter den Völkern, die sie bekehren wollten, bereits wohl fundiert waren.
Die Ähnlichkeit der Motive ist oft überraschend. Das Lothringer Doppelkreuz, das eine Wand einer katholischen Kirche in Frankreich schmückt, gleicht der Bemalung eines Sioux-Schildes in den Smithsonian-Sammlungen in Washington. Gelegentlich erzeugt die Ähnlichkeit von Zeichen mit unterschiedlicher symbolischer Bedeutung jedoch einige Verwirrung (siehe Taylor, 1994 (a): 62-63).
Sitting Bull hielt das Kruzifix von Father De Smet hoch in Ehren. Es ist dokumentiert, dass er es in den folgenden Jahren bei mehreren Gelegenheiten trug, so etwa auf dem Foto, das sein Freund D. F. Barry 1885 aufnahm, etwa 17 Jahre nach Sitting Bulls erstem Treffen mit De Smet (Abb. 2). Zugleich bestehen aber auch kaum Zweifel, dass er sich nicht zum katholischen oder einem anderen christlichen Glauben bekannte. Es war eher so, dass Sitting Bull das Kruzifix trug und respektierte, weil es ihm von einem heiligen Mann einer fremden Kultur gegeben worden war, dem er offensichtlich traute und den er achtete.[9]

years, such as in the photograph taken by his friend, D. F. Barry, in 1885, some seventeen years after Sitting Bull's first meeting with De Smet (Fig. 2). The evidence, however, is strong that he did not embrace the Catholic – or any other Christian – faith: rather, Sitting Bull probably wore the crucifix and held it in high regard, because it was given to him by a holy man of an alien race who he evidently both trusted and respected.[9]

Figure 2 Sitting Bull wearing a crucifix circa 1885. This crucifix was said to have been given to Sitting Bull in 1868 by Father De Smet. It was symbolic of the hope (which both men shared) that the Great Mystery would bring security and peace to the Sioux. Photograph by D. F. Barry.

Abb. 2 Sitting Bull mit einem Kruzifix, ca. 1885. Angeblich wurde Sitting Bull dieses Kruzifix 1868 von Father De Smet geschenkt. Es symbolisierte die Hoffnung (die beide Männer teilten), daß das Große Geheimnis den Sioux Sicherheit und Frieden bringen würde. Foto von D. F. Barry.

Sitting Bulls Rückzug nach Kanada 1877

Die 17 Jahre nach Sitting Bulls erstem Treffen mit Father De Smet waren ereignisreich. Am 25. Juni 1876 wurden Custer und dessen Kommando vernichtet - Custers letzte Schlacht. Kurz danach suchte Sitting Bull mit etwa 2.000 seiner Leute Zuflucht im Land der Grossmutter - Kanada. Hier lebten die Sioux für etwa fünf Jahre in der Region von Wood Mountain und Cypress Hills im südlichen Saskatchewan in relativem Frieden mit ihren einstigen Feinden, den Blackfeet, Cree, Assiniboin und Métis, sowie mit den kanadischen Behörden. Die kanadische Geschichte verdankt diese Episode der Diplomatie und Ehrenhaftigkeit von Personen wie Walsh, Irvine und anderen von der North-West Mounted Police, sowie Crowfoot, dem Häuptling der Blackfeet, und nicht zuletzt Sitting Bull selbst, der die vertriebenen Sioux mit grosser Autorität zusammenhielt. Den Kanadiern wäre es lieber gewesen, wenn sie zurück in ihre Heimat gegangen wären. Es gab viele Diskusionen zwischen Ottawa und London über dieses Problem. Die Besonnenheit der Behörden hielt jedoch einige Zeit vor.
Als das Parlament in Ottawa über die Kosten für den Unterhalt der

Sitting Bull's Retreat to Canada in 1877

Much happened in those seventeen years after Sitting Bull's first meeting with Father De Smet. June 25, 1876, saw the annihilation of Custer and his immediate command – Custer's Last Stand. Shortly after, Sitting Bull together with some two thousand of his people, sought refuge in the grandmother's land – Canada. Here, for almost five years, in the region of Wood Mountain and Cypress Hills of southern Saskatchewan, the Sioux lived in relative peace with former enemies, Blackfeet, Cree, Assiniboin and Métis, as well as Canadian authorities. This episode in Canadian history, is a tribute to the diplomacy and honest efforts during the interaction between individuals such as Walsh, Irvine and others of the North-West Mounted Police, Crowfoot chief of the Blackfeet and not least, Sitting Bull himself who held great sway amongst the displaced Sioux. The Canadians dearly wanted them to go back home and there was much debate, both in Ottawa and London, regarding the problem of these refugee people. Good humour by the authorities, however, prevailed for some time. Thus, when the House of Commons in Ottawa discussed the expense of looking after the Sioux whilst they

Sioux diskutierte, bemerkte Sir John A. Macdonald für die Opposition: "Ich sehe nicht, wie ein sitzender Büffel eine Grenze überqueren kann." Und der Premierminister Mackenzie erwiderte im gleichen Ton: "Nicht, ohne dass er sich erhebt." (MacEwan, 1973: 110) Im Laufe der Zeit wurde aber der Druck auf Sitting Bull, in die USA zurückzukehren, stärker. Anfang der 1880er Jahre verringerte sich die Zahl der Bisons auf den kanadischen Plains rapide. Der Besuch einer von General Terry angeführten Kommission aus den USA im Oktober 1877, um Sitting Bull zur Rückkehr zu überreden, scheiterte, obwohl zu dieser Zeit schon klar war - und das war Sitting Bull gesagt worden -, dass er nicht persönlich für die Niederlage Custers verantwortlich gemacht werden würde.

Bedeutsamer war jedoch - soweit Sitting Bulls religiöse Empfindungen betroffen waren - der Besuch von Father Martin Marty (Abb. 3), der später Bischof von South Dakota wurde. Marty drängte Sitting Bull zur Rückkehr, aber Sitting Bull lehnte dies ab, da er überzeugt war, dass die Amerikaner tatsächlich nie einen Gott anerkannt hätten, anderenfalls hätten sie niemals so viele Indianer getötet.[10] Dass Marty gesagt hatte, er komme mit Gottes Wort, löste eher Besorgnis bei ihm aus. "Gott hat mich geheissen zu kommen und dir zu verkünden...",

were in Canada, Sir John A. Macdonald for the opposition, interjected a light comment, 'I do not see how a Sitting Bull can cross a frontier' and Prime Minister Mackenzie replied in similar vein, 'Not unless he rises'! (MacEwan, 1973:110).
As time passed, Sitting Bull was subjected to increasing pressure to return to the United States. By the early 1880s, the buffalo were rapidly dwindling on the Canadian Plains. A visit from the U.S.A. by a commission headed by General Terry in October 1877, failed to persuade Sitting Bull to return to the United States even though by this time it was realized – and Sitting Bull was told this – that he could not be held personally responsible for Custer's defeat.
More significant, however, as far as Sitting Bull's religious perceptions were concerned, was the visit by Father Martin Marty (Fig. 3), who was later to become Bishop of South Dakota. Marty urged Sitting Bull to return but Sitting Bull retorted that it was his belief that the Americans really had never discovered a God, otherwise they would never had killed so many Indians.[10] He expressed concern that Marty had told him that he had come with the words of God... 'God told me to come and tell you', Marty had said and yet Sitting Bull said, 'You know....that they tried to kill me'

Figure 3 The Catholic missionary Father Martin Marty, who visited Sitting Bull in Canada. He was unsuccessful in his attempts to convert Sitting Bull to Catholicism.

Abb. 3 Der katholische Missionar Father Martin Marty, der Sitting Bull in Kanada besuchte. Er scheiterte bei dem Versuch, Sitting Bull zum Katholizismus zu bekehren.

hatte Marty gesagt. Sitting Bull erklärte: "Du weisst ..., dass sie versucht haben, mich umzubringen." Er fügte hinzu, dass die Soldaten alle töten würden, wenn die Sioux zurückkehrten. Ob der Bischof das wolle? (Manzione, 1991: 50) Sitting Bull hatte offensichtlich wenig Vertrauen in diesen religiösen Führer, der anscheinend die Tatsachen verdrehte, wie es ihm passte. Wer konnte Sitting Bull dafür tadeln, wenn ein Zeitgenosse über ihn sagte, er sei "ein starker Gegner des Christentums" (MacEwan, 1973: 166). Beschämt zog Martin Marty sich zurück und riet den Sioux schliesslich, in Kanada zu bleiben. Falls Sitting Bull aber jemals in die Vereinigten Staaten zurückzukehren wünsche, fügte er hinzu, werde er mit seinem eigenen Leben dafür bürgen, dass Freiheit und Leben der Sioux sicher seien. Es deutet einiges darauf hin, dass Sitting Bull wegen dieses Schwurs und späterer Handlungen Martys Taktlosigkeiten übersah. Es entging ihm sicher nicht, dass Marty bemerkenswerte Bemühungen unternahm, das Los der vertriebenen Sioux zu verbessern. Zwei Jahre später besuchte Marty die Sioux abermals und zeichnete ein trostloses Bild von Hunger und Krankheit in Kanada. Dagegen verwies er auf die "glänzende Situation" auf amerikanischen Reservationen (Manzione, 1991: 137).

and added that if they did return, the soldiers would kill them all. Did the Bishop, 'want that to happen?' (Manzione, 1991:50). Clearly, Sitting Bull had little faith in this religious leader who seemingly distorted things at will. Who could blame Sitting Bull, when one contemporary at the time reported that he – Sitting Bull – was 'very opposed to Christianity' (MacEwan, 1973:166).
Shamed, Martin Marty retracted and he subsequently advised the Sioux to stay in Canada but added that if Sitting Bull ever did want to return to the United States, he would pledge his own life that the liberties and lives of the Sioux would be safe. There is some evidence to suggest that, because of this pledge and later actions, Sitting Bull subsequently overlooked Marty's indiscretions; certainly, he would have been aware that Marty made further considerable efforts to improve the lot of the refugee Sioux. Two years later Marty again visited with the Sioux, painting a bleak picture of starvation and disease in Canada and contrasted it with 'the 'bright optimism' on the American reservations' (Manzione, 1991:137).

Kriegsgefangene

Durch den Entzug der Lebensmittelversorgung gezwungen und besorgt um das Wohlergehen seiner ältesten Tochter, ritt Sitting Bull schliesslich mit 187 Gefolgsleuten nach Fort Buford, wo er sich am 20. Juli 1881 Major David H. Brotherton ergab. Sein sechsjähriger Sohn Crowfoot - benannt zu Ehren des Blackfoot-Häuptlings - übergab Sitting Bulls Winchester an Major Brotherton. "Ich wünsche, dass man sich daran erinnert", sagte Sitting Bull, "dass ich der letzte Mann meines Stammes bin, der sein Gewehr abgibt" (Ewers, 1956: 21; Hedren, 1997: 20). Zwölf Tage später, am 1. August 1881, legte das Dampfschiff "General Sherman" bei Fort Yates an. Sitting Bull weinte hemmungslos, als sein Freund Running Antelope an Bord kam, um ihn zu begrüssen. "Es ist das erste Mal, dass ich kapitulieren und aufgeben musste", klagte Sitting Bull (Hedren, 1997: 35). Verschlimmert wurde die Situation durch den Umstand, dass seine geliebte Tochter Many Horses nirgends zu sehen war. Running Antelope legte seinen Arm um den Freund und sagte: "Bruder, weine nicht. Alles wird gut werden" (ibid.). Die Dinge entwickelten sich jedoch nicht wie erwartet. Statt sich auf seinem alten Heimatgebiet am Grand River niederlassen zu können, wurde

Prisoners of War

Ultimately, virtually starved into submission and anxious as to the welfare of his eldest daughter, Sitting Bull, together with one hundred and eighty-seven followers, rode into Fort Buford where they surrendered to Major David H. Brotherton on 20 July, 1881. His six year old son, Crowfoot (named in honour of the Blackfeet chief), was directed to take up Sitting Bull's Winchester and present it to Major Brotherton. 'I wish it to be remembered', Sitting Bull said, 'that I was the last man of my tribe to surrender my rifle' (Ewers, 1956:21, Hedren, 1997:20). Twelve days later, on 1 August 1881, the steamboat 'General Sherman', docked at Fort Yates. Sitting Bull wept uncontrollably when his friend, Running Antelope, went aboard to greet him. 'This is the first time I have had to surrender and give up', Sitting Bull lamented (Hedren, 1997:35). The situation was further aggravated by the fact that his beloved daughter, Many Horses, was nowhere to be seen. Running Antelope put an arm around his friend and said, 'Brother don't weep, everything will come out all right' (ibid.). Things did not, however, turn out as expected. Instead of settling back on his original homeland on the

Sitting Bull zusammen mit seinen unmittelbaren Begleitern nach Fort Randall überstellt, etwa 200 Meilen weiter südlich am Missouri. Hier wurden sie bis zum Mai 1883 als Kriegsgefangene festgehalten.[11]
Die Zeit, die sie dort verbrachten, war nicht völlig unglücklich. Viele der Offiziere wurden zu persönlichen Freunden und erkannten das grosse Unrecht an, das den Indianern geschehen war. "Ich bewunderte (ihre) Geduld und ihren Langmut", schrieb Lieutenant Colonel Ahern (Vestal, 1957: 238). Ahern, ein Linguist, war für Sitting Bull persönlich verantwortlich. Er half ihm bei der Bewältigung der Post, die ihn von Verehrern aus der ganzen Welt erreichte.[12]
Während dieses Aufenthalts war Sitting Bull erneut der christlichen Religion ausgesetzt, da er von vielen Missionaren besucht wurde. Sie lasen ihm Abschnitte aus der Bibel vor und erzählten ihm von Christus. Er dachte über die Parallelen des Glaubens nach, scheint aber persönlich zu dem Schluss gelangt zu sein, dass die Sioux wahrscheinlich die besseren "Christen" waren, bevor sie jemals von Christus gehört hatten. Jedenfalls waren sie ehrlicher in ihrem Glauben als die meisten Weissen, die er kannte. Religion basierte, wie er sagte, auf dem richtigen menschlichen Tun und nicht nur auf dem Reden darüber.

Grand River, Sitting Bull – together with his immediate followers – was transferred to Fort Randall, some two hundred miles farther south on the Missouri River: here, they were held as prisoners of war until May 1883.[11]
The time they spent there was not altogether an unhappy one. Many of the officers became personal friends, recognizing the great wrongs done to the Indian. 'I marvelled at [their] patience and forbearance!' wrote Lieutenant Colonel Ahern (Vestal, 1957:238). Ahern, a linguist, was assigned as Sitting Bull's personal guardian; and he helped Sitting Bull with the mail which he received from admirers throughout the world.[12]
It was during this sojourn, that Sitting Bull was again exposed to the Christian religion, many missionaries coming to see him. They read sections from the Bible and told him things about Christ. He mused on the parallels in their beliefs but seems to have personally concluded that the Sioux were probably better 'Christians' before they ever heard of Christ. Certainly, they were more genuine in their beliefs than most of the white people he knew! Religion, he said, was based on doing things that humans knew were right and not just something one talks about.

Eine Robe für den Papst

Möglicherweise bemalte er zu dieser Zeit eine Bisonrobe für Papst Leo XIII. Sie zeigte Sitting Bull mit einer Lanze bewaffnet im Kampf gegen Feinde, sowie bei der Erbeutung von Pferden. In der Nähe der Mitte waren Frauen in Gruppen zu sehen, und weiter im Inneren hatten sich Krieger zum Rat versammelt. Das alles gruppierte sich um ein Zentrum, in dem ein stehender Bischof gezeigt wurde, mit Sitting Bull zu seiner Linken, der ein Calumet überreichte. Böse Geister flohen entsetzt, so wurde berichtet, durch die Gegenwart des Priesters. Leider waren jahrelange Untersuchungen im Vatikan erfolglos, diese interessante Robe zu lokalisieren. Abb. 4 zeigt eine Rekonstruktion, die auf einer Beschreibung von 1885 basiert, als die Robe sich auf dem Weg nach Rom befand und in Paris ausgestellt wurde. Die Robe wurde von niemand anderem als Martin Marty befördert, dem bereits früher erwähnten guten Bekannten Sitting Bulls. Vermutlich war es Marty, der überlieferte, dass die Robe ein Zeugnis der Bekehrung Sitting Bulls zum Christentum war. Angesichts der Skepsis, die Sitting Bull der Religion des weissen Mannes gegenüber hegte, ist dies jedoch höchst unwahrscheinlich. Eher unterstreicht die Mittelpiktographie

A Robe for the Pope

It is possible that at about this time, he painted a buffalo robe for Pope Léon XIII. This showed Sitting Bull armed with a lance, in battle against enemies as well as capturing horses. Towards the centre, was a depiction of women standing in groups and closer-in were warriors in war council. All surrounded a central subject, consisting of a standing bishop with Sitting Bull at his left, presenting a calumet. Bad spirits flee frightened, it was reported, by the presence of the Black Robe. Unfortunately, researches at the Vatican over the years, have failed to locate this interesting robe. Fig. 4 is a reconstruction based on a description penned in 1885 when the robe, *en route* to Rome, was put on display in Paris. The robe was being transferred by none other than Martin Marty, a close associate of Sitting Bull, referred to earlier. There is reference to the fact, presumably related by Marty, that the robe was a monument to the conversion of Sitting Bull to Christianity. However, on the basis of Sitting Bull's known scepticism towards the white man's religion, this is highly unlikely. Perhaps the central pictograph gives equal weight to the powers of the calumet and the cross in initiating religious concepts. Whatever, it probably was produced

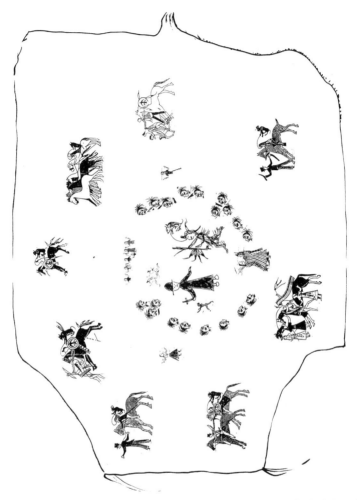

Figure 4 A reconstructed image of the robe destined for the Pope in Rome. Described as being painted by Sitting Bull and the central figures showing his conversion to Catholicism, it was put on display in Paris by Father Martin Marty in 1885. Courtesy, Paul Ritner and Peter Bowles.

Abb. 4 Eine Rekonstruktion der Robe, die für den Papst in Rom bestimmt war. Beschreibungen zufolge war sie von Sitting Bull bemalt worden, und die Mittelfiguren zeigen seine Konvertierung zum Katholizismus. Sie war 1885 in Paris durch Father Martin Marty ausgestellt worden. Mit Genehmigung von Paul Ritner und Peter Bowles.

die gleichgewichtige Bedeutung des Calumets und des Kreuzes in den grundlegenden religiösen Konzepten.

Wie auch immer: Die Robe wurde wahrscheinlich von Sitting Bull - oder jemandem, der ihm nahestand - gefertigt. Die Datenangaben stimmen, der Name des Boten ist absolut plausibel - Marty war gebürtiger Schweizer -, und der besondere Hinweis auf den Gebrauch der Lanze durch die Heldengestalt auf der Robe passt gut zu der bekannten Tatsache, dass die Lanze Sitting Bulls bevorzugte Waffe war. Die allgemeine Anordnung stimmt ebenfalls mit bekannten Sioux-Roben überein, die häufig eine zentrale Gestalt darstellten, wie etwa die Robe, die Sitting Bull dem Posttrader Gus Hedderich schenkte. Es war eine Art "Danksagung" für viele Freundlichkeiten ... nicht zuletzt dafür, dass Hedderich Sitting Bull lehrte, seinen Namen zu schreiben. (Diese Fähigkeit wurde später eine ertragreiche Einnahmequelle für Sitting Bull.) Die Hedderich-Robe befindet sich heute in den Sammlungen der State Historical Society von North Dakota in Bismarck. Es handelt sich um die Haut einer Bisonkuh, die von Sitting Bull geschossen und von seinen Frauen gegerbt wurde. Im Mittelpunkt steht das Motiv einer berstenden Sonne, und interessanterweise sind - wie

by Sitting Bull (or by someone who knew him well): the dates are right, the name of the carrier perfectly plausible – Marty was of Swiss origin – and the specific reference to the use of a lance by the hero depicted on the robe, ties in well with the known fact that the lance was Sitting Bull's favourite weapon. The general layout also conforms to known Sioux robes which not infrequently depicted a central figure such as on the robe which was given by Sitting Bull to the Post Trader, Gus Hedderich. It was by way of a 'thank you' for many kindnesses….not least the fact that Hedderich taught Sitting Bull how to sign his name. (That ability became a valuable source of income to Sitting Bull in later years). The Hedderich robe is now in the collections of the State Historical Society of North Dakota in Bismarck. It is that of a cow buffalo, the animal being shot by Sitting Bull and the hide tanned by his wives. A sunburst motif is painted at the centre and, interestingly, as with the robe sent to the Pope, there are painted calumets below which is a warrior in a horned bonnet, embellished with double trails of eagle feathers. Two birds are depicted near the head of the robe, possibly representing Spirit Messengers (Sitting Bull often listened to his bird and animal friends).[13] The

Figure 5 Sitting Bull, taken in Pierre (present-day South Dakota) when Sitting Bull and his followers were *en route* as prisoners of war from Fort Randall. Note the butterfly (a monarch?) on his hat. Butterflies, moths and cocoons evoked much Sioux religious symbolism. Photograph by R. L. Kelly. 1883.

Abb. 5 Sitting Bull, 1883. Das Bild wurde in Pierre (heute in South Dakota) aufgenommen, als Sitting Bull und seine Anhänger als Kriegsgefangene auf dem Weg nach Fort Randall waren. Man beachte den Schmetterling (ein Monarch?) an seinem Hut. Schmetterlinge, Motten und Kokons beschworen den religiösen Symbolismus der Sioux. Foto von R. L. Kelly, 1883.

auf der Robe, die dem Papst geschickt wurde - unterhalb einer Kriegergestalt mit gehörnter Haube und doppelter Federschleppe Calumets zu sehen. Unweit des Kopfes der Robe sind zwei Vögel dargestellt, möglicherweise repräsentieren sie Geisterboten. (Sitting Bull lauschte oft seinen gefiederten und anderen tierischen Freunden.)[13] Bei dem Krieger könnte es sich um Sitting Bull selbst in der Ausrüstung des "Starke-Herzen-Bundes" handeln. Sicherlich ist die unübliche Vorderansicht des Gesichts im Stil Sitting Bulls, eine Technik, die er in mehreren gut dokumentierten Piktographien anwandte. (Siehe Anhang II bezüglich einer detaillierten Erörterung der Papst-Robe.)

Endlich Daheim!

Im Mai 1883 wurden Sitting Bull und seine Leute endlich zurück auf die Standing Rock Reservation gebracht. Obwohl er nie wirklich daran interessiert war, genoss dieser grosse geistige Führer eine bemerkenswerte Prominenz. Während der nächsten Jahre - abgesehen von den offensichtlichen Spannungen zwischen ihm und dem Agenten McLaughlin - führte er ein interessantes und respektiertes Leben. Alsbald wurde ihm erlaubt, auf Reisen zu gehen und sich sogar für

warrior may be a depiction of Sitting Bull himself in Strong Heart Society regalia. Certainly, the unusual full face is a Sitting Bull style, a technique which he uses in several well documented pictographs. (See Appendix II for a more detailed discussion of the 'Pope' robe).

Back Home at Last!

Finally, in May 1883, Sitting Bull and his people were transferred back to the Standing Rock Reservation. Although he never really sought it, this great spiritual leader received very considerable prominence and during the next several years – except for the obvious tensions between him and agent McLaughlin – he lived an interesting, accommodating life. He was soon allowed to travel and even joined William F. Cody's Wild West Show for a season; but he always returned to his beloved Grand River on the Standing Rock Reservation, not far from where he was born, in what was obviously perceived as those free and happy days of long ago.[14]
In the spring of 1884, Sitting Bull was in St. Paul, Minnesota. Here again, he met Bishop Marty and other Catholic leaders. He visited the Catholic Cathedral, being greatly impressed with the enormous organ and he took a particular interest in a

eine Saison der Wild West Show William F. Codys anzuschliessen. Stets aber kehrte er zu seinem geliebten Grand River auf der Standing Rock Reservation zurück, nicht weit von dem Platz, an dem er geboren wurde. Hier fühlte er sich offensichtlich an jene freien und glücklichen Tage erinnert, die so lange vergangen waren.[14]

Im Frühjahr 1884 hielt sich Sitting Bull in St. Paul (Minnesota) auf. Hier traf er wieder auf Bischof Marty und andere katholische Führer. Er besuchte die katholische Kathedrale und war höchst beeindruckt von der riesigen Orgel, und er zeigte sich besonders an einer Jesus-Statue interessiert. Verschiedene Fotos, die zu dieser Zeit aufgenommen wurden, zeigen Sitting Bull, wie er bestimmte Elemente der religiösen Konzepte der Sioux demonstriert. Etwa in Abb. 5: Hier trägt er an seinem Hut einen Monarch-Schmetterling, das Symbol der Sioux für Regeneration und Schönheit. (Ein Schmetterling schlüpft aus einem scheinbar leblosen Kokon. Er beschwört ein Netzwerk von komplexen symbolischen Überlegungen.)[15]

Bei anderen Gelegenheiten deutet sich an, dass er es den verschiedenen Bischöfen, die er traf, nachtun wollte: Das schwarze seidene Taschentuch, das er in Abb. 6 um den Hals trägt, gibt ihm ein

statue of Jesus. Various photographs taken at this time, show Sitting Bull expressing definite elements of Sioux religious concepts – such as shown in Fig. 5, where he displays on his hat, a butterfly (Monarch?) symbolic to the Sioux of regeneration and beauty – a butterfly emerges from an apparent lifeless cocoon. It evokes a web of complex symbolic thought.[15]

At other times, there is just a hint of emulation of the various bishops that he met; the black silk handkerchief pinned close around the neck in Fig. 6, gives him a decided clerical look. He also, like the bishops, wore a large cameo ring on which was cut a cherub. However, unlike the bishops who wore their rings on the third finger of the right hand, his was worn on the middle finger of his left hand. Left-handedness, we should note, was a decided Sioux trait, used by them in religious ceremonial and symbology. Such statements of his religious convictions were not much different to the priests' robes – they were, however, more subtle.

The Ghost Dance and Death of Sitting Bull

In the late 1880s, Sitting Bull was turned to for advice and leadership in the Ghost Dance movement. In his usual manner, he considered this

entschieden klerikales Aussehen. Wie die Bischöfe schmückte er sich ebenfalls mit einem grossen Ring mit Gemme, auf dem ein Cherub eingeschnitten war. Anders als die Bischöfe, die ihre Ringe am dritten Finger der rechten Hand trugen, hatte er seinen jedoch auf den Mittelfinger der linken Hand gesteckt. Linkshänder zu sein war, wie bemerkt werden soll, eine bedeutsame Charakteristik der Sioux, die von ihm auch im religiösen Zeremoniell und in der Symbologie genutzt wurde. Derartige Zeugnisse seiner religiösen Überzeugung unterschieden sich nicht sonderlich von den Priesterroben, sie waren jedoch subtiler.

Der Geistertanz und der Tod Sitting Bulls

Ende der 1880er Jahre wurde Sitting Bull um Rat und Führung in der Geistertanzbewegung gebeten. Wie für ihn typisch, bedachte er diesen neuen religiösen Eifer mit Vorsicht. Diese Bewegung basierte unzweifelhaft auf einigen christlichen Elementen. Ihr Begründer, Wovoka, war stark weissen Einflüssen unterworfen, und die "Himmelsleiter"-Idee wurde von weissen Missionaren - wie De Smet und Lacombe - eingeführt.[16] Sitting Bull war skeptisch und bat den Agenten McLaug-

new religious fervour with caution. It was clearly based on several Christian concepts; *Wovoka*, its founder for example, had been subjected to much white influence and the 'ladder to heaven' idea was an invention of the white missionaries, such as De Smet and Lacombe.[16] Sitting Bull was sceptical and applied to agent McLaughlin for leave from the reservation to investigate it further; leave was refused. The rest is a bizarre and shameful history. In all, Sitting Bull lived nine more years after his capitulation at Fort Buford. Then he was brutally slain near his home on the Grand River, some forty miles southwest of Fort Yates. His teenage son, Crowfoot, who had tendered his father's Winchester carbine to Major Brotherton, died with him.

Sitting Bull, it is reported, was said to have had a premonition of his forthcoming death and on the hill above Grand River, he went to pray on the evening of December 14, 1890. Several of the survivors of the Indian Police who were sent to arrest Sitting Bull on the orders of Major McLaughlin, never forgave themselves for the deed. As one policeman, High Eagle, exclaimed: 'Well, we have gone to work, and killed our chief!' (Diessner, 1993:141). Red Tomahawk, who lived until 1932 and was second in command, wept when he related the

Figure 6 Sitting Bull in Montreal in 1885. The clerical type aspect of this photograph is enhanced by the black silk handkerchief pinned close around the neck. One observer has described this portrait as "Sitting Bull, as the great religious teacher" (Smith, 1943: 198). Photograph by William Norman, Montreal, Canada 1885.

Abb. 6 Sitting Bull in Montreal, 1885. Der klerikale Aspekt dieses Fotos wird durch das schwarze Seidentaschentuch verstärkt, das um seinen Hals gewunden ist. Ein Beobachter beschrieb dieses Portrait als "Sitting Bull, als der große religiöse Lehrer". (Smith, 1943: 198.) Foto von William Norman, Montreal, Kanada, 1885.

hlin, die Reservation verlassen zu dürfen,um weitere Informationen einzuholen. Dies wurde abgelehnt. Was folgte ist eine bizarre und beschämende Geschichte. Insgesamt überlebte Sitting Bull seine Kapitulation in Fort Buford 9 Jahre. Dann wurde er bei seinem Haus am Grand River, etwa 40 Meilen südwestlich von Fort Yates, brutal erschlagen. Sein Sohn Crowfoot, noch keine zwanzig Jahre, der die Winchester seines Vaters an Major Brotherton übergeben hatte, starb mit ihm.

Es wird berichtet, dass Sitting Bull eine Vorahnung von seinem bevorstehenden Tod hatte. Am Abend des 14. Dezember 1890 begab er sich auf den Hügel über dem Grand River um zu beten. Mehrere Überlebende der Indianerpolizei, die auf Befehl Major McLaughlins Sitting Bull verhaften sollten, konnten sich ihre Tat nie verzeihen. Wie einer der Polizisten, High Eagle, ausrief: "Wir mussten unsere Arbeit tun und töteten unseren Häuptling." (Diessner, 1993: 141) Red Tomahawk, der bis 1932 lebte und stellvertretender Kommandant war, weinte, wenn er über das tragische Ereignis berichtete, das durch religiösen Eifer ausgelöst wurde, der grösstenteils einer fremden Kultur entstammte.[17] Die toten Polizisten wurden innerhalb des katholischen Friedhofes christlich bestattet. Nicht so Sitting

tragic event – which was initiated by religious fervour, largely embedded in an alien culture.[17]

The dead policemen were given Christian burials – interred in the Catholic cemetery. Not so with Sitting Bull, whose body was handed over to the army and, without any religious ceremonial, red or white, buried in a corner of the military cemetery. (Recently, however, I learned that prayers were said for Sitting Bull at the time by Father Bernard Strassmeier, who had become a friend at Standing Rock.)

Marker at Grand River

Young Crowfoot and his six companions, some of Sitting Bull's closest friends, were later buried (virtually where they fell) by the Congregationalist, the Rev. Thomas Riggs. Later, at Mary Collins' instigation, a marker was put over their graves. Ironically, the words carved on it derive from yet another component of the Christian religion (Corinthians I.13:13), '…faith, hope, charity, these three; but the greatest of these is charity'. Certainly, a lot of that was needed at Standing Rock with the lives of more than a dozen families devastated by the events that occurred on the morning of 15 December, 1890. It is interesting to note, incidentally, in Fig. 7, the

Bull, dessen Leiche der Armee übergeben wurde. Er wurde ohne jegliche religiöse Zeremonie - weder indianisch noch weiss - in einer Ecke des Militärfriedhofs begraben. (Erst kürzlich erfuhr ich jedoch, dass Father Bernard Strassmeier, der auf Standing Rock sein Freund geworden war, Gebete für Sitting Bull sprach.)

Gedenktafel am Grand River

Der junge Crowfoot und seine 6 Begleiter, einige von Sitting Bulls engsten Freunden, wurde später von dem Congregationalisten Reverend Thomas Riggs beerdigt (dort wo sie gefallen waren). Später wurde auf Anregung von Mary Collins über ihren Gräbern eine Gedenktafel aufgestellt. Ironischerweise beziehen sich die Worte, die darauf eingraviert sind, auf noch eine andere Komponente der christlichen Religion (Korinther I.13: 13): "Glaube, Hoffnung, Liebe, diese drei, aber das Grösste ist Liebe."
Sicherlich wurde eine Menge davon auf Standing Rock benötigt, wo das Leben von mehr als einem Dutzend Familien durch die Ereignisse am Morgen des 15. Dezember 1890 zerstört wurden. Es ist, nebenbei erwähnt, von Interesse (Abb. 7), dass die Steine, die kürzlich am Fuss stones recently placed at the base of the marker, painted and decorated to identify them as sacred.

Sitting Bull Today

But the spirit of Sitting Bull – more than of any others red or white – lives on. As one recent biographer wrote on his visit to Grand River, 'You can feel it everywhere' (Diessner, 1993:172). Certainly there is great and increasing interest in this unusual man. The site of Sitting Bull's last campsite and last Sun Dance before he left Canada – at Quepple and Wood Mountain – have been found and wild horses in Theodore Roosevelt National Park have recently been identified as probably descended from the horses confiscated by the military, from Sitting Bull's band after he surrendered at Fort Buford. The wagon that carried his body to Fort Yates has been found. There is now a Sitting Bull College at Fort Yates and his name is greatly honoured there. Religious and other ceremonials on a small scale, are now performed annually on the Grand River, near the site where he was killed. Astoundingly, within the last year, Sitting Bull's scalp-lock – a symbol of the owner's spirit – has been found, cut off by the surgeon who prepared his body for burial.[18]

Figure 7 Grave marker to Crowfoot and the six Hunkpapa Indians – son and friends of Sitting Bull – who were killed on December 15, 1890 when attempts were made to arrest Sitting Bull by the Indian Police. Note the stones at the base of the marker, recently decorated and painted to identify them as sacred. Grand River, South Dakota. Photograph courtesy R. Gralewski.

Abb. 7 Grabstein für Crowfoot und die sechs Hunkpapa-Indianer - für den Sohn und die Freunde Sitting Bulls -, die am 15. Dezember 1890 bei dem Versuch der Indianerpolizei, Sitting Bull zu verhaften, getötet wurden. Auffällig die Steine am Fuß des Markers, erst kurz vorher verziert und bemalt, um sie als sakral zu kennzeichnen. Grand River, South Dakota. Foto mit Genehmigung von R. Gralewski.

der Gedenktafel plaziert wurden, bemalt und dekoriert sind, um sie als sakral zu kennzeichnen.

Sitting Bull heute

Der Geist Sitting Bulls - mehr als jedes anderen roten oder weissen Menschen - lebt. Wie ein neuerer Biograph über seinen Besuch am Grand River schrieb: "Man fühlt ihn überall" (Diessner, 1993: 172). Zudem gibt es ein grosses und wachsendes Interesse an diesem ungewöhnlichen Mann. Das Gelände von Sitting Bulls letztem Lagerplatz und das seines letzten Sonnentanzes, bevor er Kanada verliess - bei Quepple und Wood Mountain - wurden aufgefunden, und die Wildpferde im Theodore-Roosevelt-Nationalpark wurden erst kürzlich als wahrscheinliche Nachkommen der Pferde identifiziert, die die Armee von Sitting Bulls Gruppe nach der Kapitulation in Fort Buford konfiszierte. Der Wagen, der seine Leiche nach Fort Yates brachte, wurde entdeckt. Es gibt heute ein Sitting Bull College in Fort Yates, und sein Name wird hier hoch in Ehren gehalten. Religiöse und andere Zeremonien finden in geringem Umfang jährlich am Grand River statt, nahe dem Platz, wo er ermordet wurde. Erstaunlicherweise wurde 1998 Sitting Bulls Skalplocke

The Sioux and Catholic Religion Today

Recently, Father Casimir Paluck at the Catholic Indian Mission at Fort Yates, told me that during the celebration of the Mass, there is now a blend of Christian and traditional Sioux religion.
The church resembles a giant tipi and a pipe and feathered headdress adorn the altar. He reports that the Sioux had and still have 'a deep concept of God's presence, God gives life and being to all ... all are related [including] the animal world and the plant world. Children are [considered] a sacred gift of God and especially honored as such... The Sioux people have a concept of God that is very much in accord with Catholic belief' (CP to CFT, February 5th 1999). Such sentiments were clearly similar to those expressed and held by Sitting Bull, more than a century ago.
Times have clearly changed from the days when Catholic missionaries and others, accused the Sioux of worshipping nothing but animals, rocks and stone! It is becoming increasingly recognized that the Sioux attitudes to spirit helpers, is close to the western attitudes towards sacred books, such as the Old and New Testaments – they were authoritative and treated with respect but not adored.[19] Likewise,

- ein Symbol des Geistes ihres Eigentümers - entdeckt, die der Militärarzt einst abgeschnitten hatte, der die Leiche für das Begräbnis vorbereitete.[18]

Die Sioux und die katholische Religion heute

Erst kürzlich erklärte mir Father Casimir Paluck von der Catholic Indian Mission in Fort Yates, dass heute bei der Messe eine Vermischung christlicher und traditioneller Sioux-Religion stattfindet. Die Kirche gleicht einem riesigen Tipi, und der Altar wird von einer Pfeife und einer Federhaube geschmückt. Er berichtet, dass die Sioux noch immer "ein starkes Gefühl für die Gegenwart Gottes" haben. "Gott verleiht allem Leben und Existenz..., alle sind miteinander verwandt, eingeschlossen die tierische und pflanzliche Welt. Kinder werden als heiliges Geschenk Gottes betrachtet und als solches besonders geehrt... Das Volk der Sioux hat ein göttliches Konzept, das sehr stark mit der katholischen Lehre übereinstimmt" (CP zu CFT, 5. Februar 1999). Solche Überlegungen ähneln jenen, die Sitting Bull über ein Jahrhundert zuvor ausdrückte und beachtete. Seit den Tagen, da die katholischen Missionare und andere die Sioux beschuldigten, lediglich Tiere,

it is more clearly understood that such objects as medicine bundles, ceremonial regalia, pipes, shields and the like, were types of 'documents' which embodied the religious concepts of the people that used them.
Recently, several authors have challenged the beliefs about Jesus and are denying some of the very cornerstones of Christianity. Thus the Australian theologian Barbara Thiering of Sidney University, not only denies the resurrection but also claims that Jesus did not die on the cross: whilst the idea of the Trinity claims the distinguished novelist A. N. Wilson, "would be laughable to Jesus who was a monotheistic Jew". Such views, however, are contested by such theologians as The Right Rev. John Taylor, Bishop of St. Albans, and Dr Dick France, a New Testament scholar and Principal of Ridley Hall, Oxford. At the same time, scientific discoveries offer support for spirituality and hints of the very nature of God. Thus Nobel Prize winner in Physics, Charles Townes of the University of California, Berkeley, believes that recent discoveries in cosmology reveal "a universe that fits religious views ... somehow intelligence must have been involved in the laws of the universe". Whilst John Polkinghorne, a Physicist turned Priest, observes that the fundamental

Felsen und Steine anzubeten, hat sich viel geändert. Es wurde zunehmend anerkannt, dass die Sicht der Sioux in Bezug auf Geisthelfer nicht weit von der westlichen Einstellung bezüglich sakraler Bücher, wie dem Alten und Neuen Testament, entfernt ist - sie waren einflussreich, man ging respektvoll mit ihnen um, aber sie wurden nicht angebetet.[19] Es wird besser verstanden, dass Objekte wie Medizinbündel, zeremonielle Ausrüstungen, Pfeifen, Schilde und ähnliches eine Art "Zeugnis" waren, eine Darstellung der religiösen Ideen des Volkes, das sie benutzte.

Erst kürzlich haben mehrere Autoren den Glauben an Jesus in Frage gestellt und einige der Eckpfeiler des Christentums verworfen. So bestreitet die australische Theologin Barbara Thiering von der Sidney University nicht nur die Wiederauferstehung, sondern behauptet auch, daß Jesus nicht am Kreuz starb, während die Vorstellung der Dreifaltigkeit - wie der angesehene Romancier A. N. Wilson - feststellte, "lachhaft für Jesus gewesen wäre, der ein monotheistischer Jude war". Solche Meinungen werden von Theologen wie The Right Reverend John Taylor, Bischof von St. Albans, und Dr. Dick France, einem neutestamentarischen Wissenschaftler und Prinzipal von Ridley Hall, Oxford, jedoch angefochten. Gleichzeitig unterstützen wissenschaftliche component of a belief in God "is that there is a mind and a purpose behind the universe".[20]

Emphasis by missionaries when they sought out leaders such as Sitting Bull for conversion to Christianity, clearly considered that they were offering a higher order of religion, denigrating others as 'primitive'. What individuals such as De Smet and Marty failed to appreciate was that the religious concepts of the Sioux were in many ways, similar to their own and also that confusion occurred with so many denominations clamouring to convert the Sioux to a particular type of Christianity – as underlined by the *echelle* teaching aids.

The rich religious ceremonialism, as understood by Sitting Bull and other keepers of the Sioux people's spirituality (and which so well matched their environment), is increasingly being recognized as much more than merely an earlier evolutionist stage. In this respect, descendants and representatives of the likes of Sitting Bull and De Smet are now, it seems, in far more accord!

Acknowledgements

For information on Martin Marty, Sitting Bull and Catholicism in North America I am particularly indebted to Father *Casimir Paluck,*

Erkenntnisse spirituelle Hinweise auf die grundsätzliche Natur Gottes. Charles Townes von der University of California in Berkeley, Nobelpreisträger für Physik, glaubt jedoch, dass kürzliche Entdeckungen in der Kosmologie "ein Universum, dass zu religiösen Ansichten paßt", offenbaren. "Irgendwie muß eine Intelligenz in die Gesetze des Universums involviert sein." Dagegen beobachtete der Physiker John Polkinghorne, der zum Priester wurde, dass die fundamentale Komponente des Glaubens an Gott ist, "dass es einen Willen und ein Ziel hinter dem Universum gibt." [20]
Die Missionare, die sich um einen Übertritt zum Christentum von Führern wie Sitting Bull bemühten, betonten ihre Überzeugung, eine höhere Form der Religion anzubieten. Anderes taten sie als "primitiv" ab.

Was Männer wie De Smet und Marty nicht erkannten war, dass die religiösen Konzepte der Sioux in vielerlei Hinsicht ihren eigenen ähnelten. Dass so viele Glaubensrichtungen sich lautstark um eine Missionierung der Sioux zu einer bestimmten Art des Christentums bemühten, sorgte für Verwirrung - wie die abgestuften Lehrhilfen unterstrichen.

Der reiche religiöse Zeremonialismus, wie Sitting Bull und andere Hüter der Spiritualität der Sioux ihn

and ***Mark Thiele*** who was generous with his time in making the *Marquette Archives* at *University of Milwaukee* accessible to me.
Thanks also to ***Phil Runkel*** Archivist at Marquette. My thanks also to ***Tom Foley*** of Dunwoody, Georgia who shared some of his research data relating to Father Craft and to ***Joelle Rostkowski*** for her help with contacts and encouragement to produce this paper.
Joseph Balmer, David Rood, Chris Sanderson and ***Mike Strong*** have been incredibly helpful with opinions and sharing thoughts relating to Sitting Bull's "true" name as discussed in Appendix I. Thanks also to ***Paula Fleming*** and ***William Sturtevant*** of the *Smithsonian Institution*, Washington D. C. who, as always, have been helpful and supportive in this piece of research as have ***Paul Ritner*** and ***Peter Bowles*** who helped with the artwork for the "Pope" robe.
Thanks again to my wife ***Betty*** who checked the quotes and the entire manuscript and helped, as always, in a dozen different ways.
Last (but by no means least), my thanks to ***Helga*** and ***Dietmar Kuegler*** who have taken great care with this paper in an attempt to add to the correct historical record.

verstanden (und der so gut mit ihrer Lebenswelt übereinstimmte) wird zunehmend als viel mehr als nur ein niedrigeres Entwicklungsstadium anerkannt. In dieser Hinsicht sind die Nachfahren und Repräsentanten solcher Menschen wie Sitting Bull und De Smet, wie es scheint, in weit grösserer Übereinstimmung.

Danksagung

Für Informationen über Father Martin Marty, Sitting Bull und den Katholizismus in Nordamerika schulde ich besonders **Mark Thiele** Dank, der mir grosszügig seine Zeit geopfert hat, um mir die *Marquette Archives* der University of Milwaukee zugänglich zu machen. Dank auch an **Phil Runkel**, Archivar in Marquette. Ausserdem danke ich **Tom Foley** aus Dunwoody, Georgia, der einige seiner Forschungsergebnisse über Father Craft mit mir teilte, sowie **Joelle Rostkowski** für ihre Hilfe bei der Herstellung von Kontakten und ihre Ermutigung, diese Studie zu erarbeiten. **Joseph Balmer, David Rood, Chris *Sanderson* und *Mike Strong*** waren außerordentlich hilfreich mit Anregungen und Überlegungen bezüglich Sitting Bulls "wahrem" Namen, wie im Anhang I erörtert. *Paula Fleming* und *William Sturtevant* von der Smithsonian Institution halfen mir und unterstützten mich - wie immer - bei diesen besonderen Recherchen. *Paul Rittner* und *Peter Bowles* halfen bei der Zeichnung der "Papst"-Robe.

Nicht zuletzt geht ein Dank wieder an meine Frau *Betty*, die die Zitate und das gesamte Manuskript prüfte, sowie wie stets in vielfältiger Weise geholfen hat.

Schließlich geht mein Dank an *Helga* und *Dietmar Kuegler*, die sich sehr darum bemüht haben, zu den historischen Aufzeichnungen beizutragen.

Anhang I
Sitting Bull oder Supreme Bull?

Einführung

Ein Hinweis auf der Lund-Konferenz auf noch laufende Untersuchungen bezüglich Sitting Bulls "korrektem" Namen als Beleg seiner Stellung insbesondere bei den eng mit ihm verbundenen Lakota-Gruppen führte zu einer umfassenden Diskussion über Lakota-Linguistik. Der Sachverhalt ist komplex. Vielleicht handelt es sich auch um ein "Spiel mit Worten", wozu die Sioux neigten. Oder reicht die Bedeutung sogar tiefer? Haben wir es mit einem anderen Beispiel einer sakralen Sprache zu tun, einer besonders in religiösen Zeremonien benutzten Sprache, für "Ritual-Spezialisten", um Religion, um die Namen von sakralen Personen oder ähnlichem? (Powers 1986 und Dahlstrom 1987)

Hintergrund des Themas

Wie bereits kurz im Hauptteil dieser Studie erwähnt, wurde meine Aufmerksamkeit auf mögliche Missverständnisse im Zusammenhang mit dem Namen "Sitting Bull" erstmals 1975 erregt, als ich auf

Appendix I
Sitting Bull or Supreme Bull?

Introduction

A reference at the Lund conference to ongoing research relating to Sitting Bull's "true" name as indicative of his standing, particularly to the Lakota groups close to him, led to considerable discussion regarding Lakota linguistics. The issue was complex, perhaps a "play on words" which the Sioux were inclined to do. Or was it something deeper? Another example of sacred language – special language used in religious ceremonies, for "ritual specialists", religion, the names of sacred beings and the like? (Powers 1986 and Dahlstrom 1987).

Background to the subject

As briefly touched on in the main body of this article, my attention was first drawn to the possible misunderstandings associated with the name "Sitting Bull" when, in 1975, I made reference to Thomas B. Marquis's assessment of Sitting Bull (Taylor 1975:81). Marquis had spoken at length to both elderly Sioux and Cheyenne Indians regarding the status of Sitting Bull. He subsequently recorded that to get a

Thomas B. Marquis Beurteilung Sitting Bulls hinwies (Taylor 1975: 81). Marquis hatte umfangreiche Gespräche mit älteren Sioux und Cheyenne über die Stellung Sitting Bulls geführt. Er stellte abschliessend fest, dass der Name, entsprechend der wahren Bedeutung dieses Mannes, etwa als "Ein Bisonbulle, der ständig unter uns lebt" übertragen werden sollte (Marquis 1934: 8). Sitting Bull genoss offensichtlich hohe Wertschätzung, was sich in einem Namen widerspiegelt, der mit dem Bison in Zusammenhang gebracht wird: eine verehrte Kreatur, die als machtvoll, weise und eng mit dem Schöpfer verbunden angesehen wird, und vor allem ein grosser Versorger.

Aufgrund meiner Veröffentlichung von 1975 erhielt ich eine Antwort des Schweizer Forschers Joseph Balmer, der über 60 Jahre lang in enger Verbindung mit den Dakota auf Standing Rock und Pine Ridge stand. Er schrieb: "Der wahre Name von Sitting Bull ist *T'at'aŋ'ka 'iyo'taŋke*, vielleicht die beste Übersetzung ist "Supreme Bull"." Balmer glaubte, dass diese der Marquis-Erklärung am nächsten kam (JB an CFT, Juni 1975).

Balmer berichtete ferner, dass dies der Name war, den alle seine früheren Briefpartner auf Standing Rock (wie Judge Francis Zahn, John Colhoff und James H. Red Cloud)

true meaning of the man's name it should be rendered something like "A Buffalo Bull Resides Permanently Among Us" (Marquis 1934:8). Great esteem was obviously accorded to Sitting Bull which was reflected in a name associated with the buffalo: an honoured creature, considered powerful, wise, close to the creator and, above all, a great provider.

My 1975 publication brought a response from the Swiss scholar Joseph Balmer who for more than sixty years was in close communication with the Dakota at Standing Rock and Pine Ridge. He wrote, "the true name of Sitting Bull is *T'at'aŋ'ka 'iyo'taŋke* perhaps the best translation being "Supreme Bull". Balmer felt that this came close to Marquis's explanation of him. (JB to CFT. June 1975). Balmer also reported that this was the name used by all his early correspondents at both Standing Rock (such as Judge Francis Zahn, John Colhoff and James H. Red Cloud) and Pine Ridge (Father Sialm) as well as Father Zimmerman at St. Francis Mission. (JB to CFT. June 1999).

Such references obviously raised several interesting points for further investigation, not least that perhaps Sitting Bull's "true" name had possibly been lost to scholarship. It was considered worthy of research

und auf Pine Ridge (Father Sialm) sowie Father Zimmermann von der St. Francis Mission benutzt hatten. (JB an CFT, Juni 1999).

Diese Hinweise werfen offensichtlich mehrere interessante Fragen für weitere Nachforschungen auf, nicht zuletzt, dass Sitting Bulls "wahrer" Name möglicherweise im Wissenschaftlichen verlorengegangen ist. Da es möglich ist, weitere Einblicke in die Persönlichkeit und den Status dieses ungemein patriotischen Führers zu gewinnen, sind weitere Nachforschungen gerechtfertigt.

Übertragungen von Sitting Bulls Namen

Eine Durchsicht der Literatur und anderer Niederschriften enthüllte eine bemerkenswerte Vielfalt bei der Übertragung von Sitting Bulls Namen, wie einige wenige Auflistungen belegen:

(i) *Tatanka Iyontanke.*
 (Inschrift über der Begräbnisstätte in Fort Yates durch die N.D.S.H.S.)

(ii) *Tatonka-e-o-tonka.*
 (Pictographs. Fort Randall. 1882).

(iii) *Tata^{n}ka Yota^{n}ka.*
 (Hodge (ed), 1910 Part 2:583).

because of the possibility of getting further insights regarding the personality and status of this highly patriotic leader.

Renderings of Sitting Bull's name

A survey of the literature and elsewhere revealed considerable variations in the rendering of Sitting Bull's name - a few will illustrate this point:-

(i) *Tatanka Iyontanke.*
 (Erected over grave site at Fort
 Yates by N.D.S.H.S.)

(ii) *Tatonka-e-o-tonka.*
 (Pictographs. Fort Randall. 1882).

(iii) *Tata^{n}ka Yota^{n}ka.*
 (Hodge (ed), 1910 Part 2:583).

(iv) *Tatanka Iyotanka.*
 (Fiske 1933:13 and Feest 1999:8).

(v) *Tatanka Iyotake.*
 (Monument at Mobridge 1953).

(vi) *Ta-tan´aka I-yo-ta´-ke.*
 (Vestal 1957:13).

(vii) *tata^{n}ka iyo take.*
 (Blish 1967:216).

(viii) *Tata^{n}ka Iyotaka.*
 (Buechel 1983:11).

(iv) *Tatanka Iyotanka.*
(Fiske 1933:13 and Feest 1999:8).

(v) *Tatanka Iyotake.*
(Monument in Mobridge 1953).

(vi) *Ta-tan'-ka I-yo-ta'-ke.*
(Vestal 1957:13).

(vii) *tata^{n}ka iyo take.*
(Blish 1967:216).

(viii)*Tata^{n}ka Iyotaka.*
(Buechel 1983:11).

(ix) *Tatanka-Iyotanka.*
(Utley 1993:5).

(x) *Tatanka Iyotaka.*
(Feest 1999:8)

(xi) *Tataŋ'ka-iyo'take.*
(Densmore 1918: 458)

Die beträchtlichen Unterschiede sind möglicherweise durch eine Vermischung von Dakota und Lakota entstanden, durch falsches Buchstabieren, durch die Niederschrift in Lautsprache - wie die Fort-Randall-Übertragung ((ii) 1882) -, oder einfach durch Desinteresse am Aufbau der Lakota-Sprache. Ferner sollte beachtet werden, dass in wenigen dieser Beispiele berücksichtigt wird, welche Silben betont werden. Müssen diese Namen alle als "Sitting Bull" verstanden

(ix) *Tatanka-Iyotanka.*
(Utley 1993:5).

(x) *Tatanka Iyotaka.*
(Feest 1999:8)

(xi) *Tataŋ'ka-iyo'take.*
(Densmore 1918: 458)

The considerable variation is possibly due to a mixture of Dakota and Lakota, bad spelling, phonetic spelling – such as the Fort Randall ((ii) 1882) rendering – or simply an indifference to the technicalities of Lakota linguistics. It should also be noted that few of these examples consider which syllables are stressed. Are they all to read "Sitting Bull" or do some actually read "Supreme Bull"? If the latter why this apparent elevated status?

Sitting Bull prior to circa 1880

The earliest insightful references to Sitting Bull extend back to the visit of Father Pierre-Jean De Smet to the Sioux in 1868. He was obviously impressed with Sitting Bull, referring to him as the "generalissimo" of the village (Carriker 1995: 223). De Smet stayed in Sitting Bull's tipi (see Appendix II). Later (circa 1869) Sitting Bull was elevated to the status of "supreme chief" by those Lakota closest to him (Utley

werden, oder bedeuten einige tatsächlich "Supreme Bull"? Falls letzteres der Fall ist, warum dieser offensichtlich erhöhte Status?

Sitting Bull vor 1880

Die ersten persönlichen Zeugnisse über Sitting Bull reichen zurück zu dem Besuch von Father Pierre-Jean De Smet bei den Sioux 1868. Offensichtlich war er von Sitting Bull beeindruckt und erwähnte ihn als "Generalissimus" des Dorfes (Carriker 1995: 223). De Smet wohnte in Sitting Bulls Tipi (siehe Anhang II). Später, ca. 1869, stieg Sitting Bull bei den Lakota, die ihm am nächsten standen, zum "obersten Häuptling" auf (Utley 1993: 87-88). Neben den bereits erwähnten Belegen über das hohe Ansehen, das Sitting Bull genoss, verfügen wir auch über das Zeugnis von E. H. Allison, der sich mit Sitting Bull 1880-81 in Kanada aufhielt (siehe Fussnote 4b). Allison erwähnt Sitting Bulls ausserordentliche Grosszügigkeit und Menschlichkeit - "ein grosser Philantroph" (Allison 1897 (a)). "Das Volk verehrte ihn in einem Masse, wie die Israeliten die Bundeslade, oder wie wir die "Stars and Stripes". Was die Bienenkönigin für ihr Volk ist, war Sitting Bull für seine Leute. Mit ihm waren sie vereinigt, ohne ihn gespalten" (ibid.). Später wies er auf die 1993: 87-88). In addition to the references already given of the high regard in which Sitting Bull was held, we also have those of E. H. Allison who was with Sitting Bull in Canada 1880-81 (see Footnote 4 (b)). Allison makes reference to Sitting Bull's great generosity and humanity – "a great philanthropist" (Allison 1897 (a)). "The people "carried him about" very much as the Israelites carried the Ark of the Covenant, or as we carry the stars and stripes. What the queen bee is to the swarm Sitting Bull was to his people, with him they were united, without him they were scattered abroad" (ibid). Later, he made reference to the fact that the Sioux language had been "sadly misinterpreted" feeling that a more correct rendering of the true meaning of Sitting Bull's name would be "The Bull in Possession", "The Conquering Bull", "The Bull of Occupation", "The Sitting Bull" (N.A.A. MS. 1755). Clearly this is close to Balmer's "Supreme Bull" version referred to earlier.

Linguistics of a name

More recent is the reference to "Sitting Bull" by the prolific linguist Ella. C. Deloria. Of Yankton Sioux origin and born in 1888, she lived and worked on the Standing Rock and Pine Ridge Reservations in the

Tatsache hin, dass die Sioux-Sprache "leider falsch übersetzt" wurde. Er war überzeugt, dass eine korrektere Übertragung der wahren Bedeutung von Sitting Bulls Namen "Besitzender Bison" sein würde. "Der erobernde Bison", "Der besitzergreifende Bison", der "Sitzende Bison" (NA, M. S. 1755). Das ist nicht weit von der Balmer-Version vom "Supreme Bull" entfernt.

Der Name in der Linguistik

Neueren Datums sind die Ausführungen der profilierten Sprachwissenschaftlerin Ella C. Deloria über Sitting Bull. Von Yankton-Sioux-Abstammung - geboren 1888 -, lebte und arbeitete sie in den 1920er und 1930er Jahren auf den Standing Rock und Pine Ridge Reservationen. Mit hohen wissenschaftlichen Fähigkeiten begabt, arbeitete sie mit Anthropologen wie Franz Boas und Ruth Benedict zusammen. Sie brachte eine bedeutende Veröffentlichung über Sioux-Grammatik heraus (Boas u. Deloria 1939). In diesem Band (S. 70) lenkt sie das Interesse auf korrekte Namensübersetzungen ins Englische als Substantive und qualifizierendes Adjektiv. Bezogen auf den Namen Sitting Bull schreibt sie: *t'at'ąka 'iyótąke* - "Supreme Bull" Diesen Namen nutzte der Linguist

1920s and 1930s. Of high academic ability, she collaborated with such anthropologists as Franz Boas and Ruth Benedict. A major publication on Sioux grammar was produced by Deloria (Boas and Deloria 1939). In that volume (p. 70) she turns attention to proper names translated in English as noun and qualifying adjective. Turning her attention to the name of Sitting Bull she writes:- *t'at'ąka 'iyótąke* – "Supreme Bull".

This name was put to the linguist David Rood who, together with Allan R. Taylor (both of the University of Colorado), wrote the chapter on Lakota for the new Handbook of North American Indians (Vol. 17 1996). He commented that Deloria's apostrophes "are in fact four different symbols, ', ', `, and an acute accent mark such as over the o (ó) and a (á). Further, Deloria uses a nasal hook ą to mark nazalization" (DR to CFT June 1999). Such symbols are not easily rendered on a typewriter. A partial solution to the problem is to use "aη" in place of a. The η Greek letter "eta" then marks nazalization.
Thus Deloria's *t'at'ąka 'iyótąke* could within reason be written as *t´at´aη´ka ´iyó taηke (T´at´aη´ka ´Iyó taηke)*. This is as Balmer rendered it, i.e. "Supreme Bull". Deloria also wrote *t'at'ąka-'i`yotake* – "he sits as a bull" or

David Rood, der zusammen mit Allan R. Taylor - beide von der University of Colorado - das Kapitel über Lakota für das neue Handbook of North American Indians (Vol. 17, 1996) schrieb, als Beispiel. Er bemerkte, dass Delorias Apostrophes "tatsächlich 4 verschiedene Symbole sind, ', ', `, und ein Akutakzent, wie etwa über dem o (ó) und dem a (á). Ferner benutzt Deloria einen Nasalhaken *ą* um die Nasalierung zu kennzeichnen" (DR an CFT, Juni 1999). Derartige Symbole sind mit einer Schreibmaschine nicht leicht zu übertragen. Eine teilweise Lösung des Problems ist die Verwendund von "aη" statt a. Der griechische Buchstabe für "eta" kennzeichnet dann den Nasallaut. Somit könnte Delorias *t'at'ąka 'iyótąke* sehr wahrscheinlich als *t'at'aη'ka 'iyó taηke (T'at'aη'ka 'Iyó taηke)* geschrieben werden. Dies bedeutet, wie von Balmer übertragen, "Supreme Bull".

Deloria schrieb auch *t'at'ąka-'i`yotake* - "Er sitzt wie wie ein Bisonbulle" oder *t'at'ąka 'íyotake* - "Sitzender Bisonbulle". Das erste könnte somit geschrieben werden als *t'at'áη'ka 'i'yotake. (T'at'aη'ka 'Iyótąke*, "Sitting Bull"). David Rood glaubte, dass "Grosser Häuptling Bisonbulle" oder "Bisonbulle, der wie ein grosser Häuptling ist" nach eingehender Analyse die "beste Widergabe" des Lakota *t'at'ą'ka t'at'ąka 'íyotake* – "bull sits". The first could thus be written as *t'at'áη'ka 'i'yotake. (T'at'aη'ka 'Iyótąke*, "Sitting Bull").

David Rood felt that "Great-Chief Bull" or "Bull who is like a great chief" might, after detailed analysis be the "best gloss" on the Lakota *"t'at'ą'ka 'iyótąke"* and had no problem with "Supreme Bull" as capturing the essence of the name (ibid.).

Adoption of the Colorado University system for the Lakota language – which is used in the new North American Indian Handbook (Vol. 17) – leads to a replacement of the first and second apostrophes with an 'q' the only awkward printing then being the 'a' with the nasal hook (*ą*) hence:-

t'at'ą́ka 'iyótąke = thatháka iyótąke
that is:- "Supreme Bull".

See Fig. 9 for a tabulation produced by David Rood for this paper. Note the closeness in the phonetics. Could it be the name was misheard, translated into Sitting Bull and then translated back to the equivalent Lakota? Could it be that, with Sitting Bull's maturity (the two names were so close anyway), emphasis was put on "Supreme"? Considering the historical record "Supreme Bull" seems more appropriate for this unusual leader – known for his independence, fierce

'iyótqke ist. Er hatte keine Probleme mit "Supreme Bull" als Konzentration auf die Essenz des Namens (ibid.).

Übernimmt man das System der Colorado University für Lakota-Sprache - das im neuen Handbook of North American Indians (Vol. 17) benutzt wird -, wird das erste und zweite Apostroph durch ein "*q*" ersetzt. Das einzige Problem der Druckwiedergabe bleibt dann das "a"mit dem nasalen Haken (*q*): *t'at'ą́ka 'iyótqke* = *thatháka iyótqke* das ist: "Supreme Bull" Abb. 9 zeigt eine von David Rood für diese Studie angefertigte Tabellierung. Man beachte die enge Verbindung in der lautschriftlichen Wiedergabe. Könnte es sein, dass der Name falsch verstanden, als "Sitting Bull" übersetzt und dann in die Lakota-Entsprechung zurückübersetzt wurde? Könnte es sein, dass in Sitting Bulls reiferen Jahren bei beiden Namen - die ohnehin eng beieinander lagen - die Betonung auf "Supreme" verlagert wurde? Berücksichtigt man seine historischen Leistungen, scheint "Supreme Bull" angemessener für diesen aussergewöhnlichen Führer, der für seine Unabhängigkeit, seinen entschiedenen Patriotismus, seine Grosszügigkeit und Menschlichkeit bekannt war. Das Namenszeichen in Sitting Bulls Piktographie und die Unterschrift "Sitting Bull" lassen noch patriotism, generosity and humanity. The name glyph used in Sitting Bull's pictograph and the signature "Sitting Bull" still raise queries – they should not be too difficult to resolve. These will be left for further debate.

Shifting away from the rigour of academic linguistics, perhaps a reference to the people themselves is appropriate as Joseph Balmer observed:-

"In English Sitting Bull is [acceptable] but when dealing with Sioux Indians and to know their own language you must have in mind, that "Supreme Buffalo" was the correct name and not "Bull sit down". We have to understand "Indian feelings"! (JB to CFT. June 1999).

immer Fragen offen. Diese sollten unschwer zu beantworten sein und einer späteren Diskussion überlassen bleiben.
Wendet man sich von der reinen akademischen Sprachforschung ab, ist vielleicht der direkte Bezug auf das Volk angemessen, wie Joseph Balmer beobachtete: *"Im Englischen ist Sitting Bull (akzeptabel), aber wenn man mit Sioux-Indianern zu tun hat und deren eigene Sprache kennt, muss man berücksichtigen, dass "Supreme Bull" der korrekte Name ist und nicht "der sich hinsetzende Bulle". Wir müssen "indianische Überzeugungen" verstehen! (JB an CFT, Juni 1999)"*

Figure 8 Sitting Bull or Supreme Bull?   Abb. 8 Sitting Bull oder Supreme Bull?

Anhang II
Eine Robe für den Papst

Einführung

Mein Interesse an einer möglicherweise von Sitting Bull bemalten Bisonrobe für Papst Leo XIII. erregte zunächst der Schriftsteller und Künstler DeCost Smith, der 1943 feststellte, dass "(Sitting Bull) um 1886 eine Bisonrobe, auf die er mit eigener Hand seine Kriegstaten gemalt hatte, als Geschenk zu keinem Geringeren als dem Papst sandte" (Smith 1943: 192). DeCost Smith hatte in den 1880er und 1890er Jahren einige Zeit auf der Standing Rock Reservation verbracht und Sitting Bull gut kennengelernt. Er notierte eine interessante, prägnante Beobachtung über den Häuptling, die einst meine Aufmerksamkeit erregte (und die ich seitdem nicht vergessen habe): "Auf seine Art liebte Sitting Bull, wie ich denke, die Menschen" (ibid: 185). Wahrscheinlich hat Smith die "Papst"-Robe nicht gesehen. Er berichtete, dass "eine kürzliche Nachforschung in den ethnologischen Sammlungen im Vatikan- und im Lateran-Museum keine Hinweise darauf erbrachten" (ibid: 192).

Appendix II
A robe for the Pope

Introduction

My attention was first drawn to the possible production of a painted buffalo robe by Sitting Bull for Pope Léon XIII, by the writer and artist DeCost Smith who, in 1943, recorded that "about the year 1886 [Sitting Bull] sent as a present to no less personage than the Pope a buffalo robe with his war exploits painted on it by his own hand." (Smith 1943:192). DeCost Smith had spent some time on the Standing Rock Reservation in the 1880s and 1890s and got to know Sitting Bull well. He made an interesting, trenchant observation on this chief which caught my attention at the time (and which has stayed with me ever since): "In his way I think Sitting Bull was a lover of humanity" (ibid 185).
It is probable that Smith had not seen the "Pope" robe, reporting that "A recent search of the ethnological collections in both the Vatican and Lateran Museums failed to reveal a trace of it" (ibid: 192).

Descriptions of the Robe

More details --- presumably unknown to Smith - of this robe had actually been published as early as 1885 in the "Revue d'Ethnographie" Vol IV, the text of which is reproduced below:-

La robe de Sitting-Bull
Mgr Martin Merry [sic], évèque et
vicaire apostolique du Dakota, est
récemment passé à Paris, porteur
d'un présent tout à fait original
envoyé au pape Léon XIII par le
fameux chef indien, Sitting-Bull.
C'est une robe en peau de bison,
monument de sa conversion au
catholicisme, exécuté suivant les
procédés traditionnels des tribus des
Prairies. On y distingue trois
bandes ou enceintes concentriques,
entourant un sujet central. La
bande extérieure nous montre
Sitting-Bull, armé généralement
d'une lance, détruisant ses ennemis,
prenant des chevaux, etc. La
seconde bande ou enceinte repré-
sente les squaws debout par
groupes. Dans la troisième sont
accroupis les guerriers du conseil.
Enfin, au milieu on voit l'évèque
debout, et à sa droite Sitting-Bull
incliné, lui présentant le calumet.
Les sorciers se sauvent, effrayés par
la présence de la Robe Noire, et
emportent avec eux les engins de
leurs sorcelleries.
                    R. De Sémallé

Eine deutsche Übersetzung dieser Beschreibung lautet:
Monsignore Martin Merry (sic), Bischof und "Vikar" von Dakota, traf kürzlich in Paris ein. Mit sich führte er ein recht ausgefallenes Geschenk von dem berühmten Indianerhäuptling Sitting Bull für Papst Leo XIII. Es handelt sich um eine Bisonhaut, ein Dokument seiner Konvertierung zum Katholizismus, die entsprechend den traditionellen Ritualen der Präriestämme vollzogen wurde. Sie zeigt 3 konzentrische Bänder oder Ringe, die eine zentrale Gestalt einschliessen. Das äussere Band zeigt uns Sitting Bull, generell mit einer Lanze bewaffnet, der seine Feinde vernichtet, Pferde erbeutet, usw. Das zweite Band zeigt in Gruppen stehende Frauen. Im dritten sind Krieger des Rates zusammengefasst. Dann sehen wir in der Mitte den stehenden Bischof und zu seiner Rechten Sitting Bull in vorgebeugter Haltung. Er bietet ein Calumet dar. Die Medizinmänner flüchten, verängstigt von der Gegenwart des Schwarzrocks, und nehmen alle ihre Hexereiwerkzeuge mit sich.

Diese Beschreibung von einigen Piktographien, die teilweise von Sitting Bull in anderem Zusammenhang gezeichnet wurden (Vestal, 1957), wurde zusammen mit einer Übertragung der zentralen Figuren von einem Künstler benutzt, um ein

An English translation of this description reads as follows:-
Mgr Martin Merry [sic], Bishop and "Vicar" of Dakota, recently came to Paris, carrying a quite original present sent to Pope Léon XIII by the famous Indian Chief, Sitting Bull. It is a robe in bison skin, monument to his conversion to Catholicism, which took place according to the traditional rituals of the Prairie tribes. There are three concentric bands or rings surrounding a central figure (subject). The outside band shows us Sitting Bull, generally armed with a lance, destroying his enemies, taking horses, etc.
The second band represents squaws standing in groups. In the third, warriors of the council are grouped. Then, in the middle we see the bishop standing, and on his right, Sitting-Bull leaning forward, offering him the calumet. The medicine men flee, terrified by the presence of the Black Robe, taking with them all their implements of sorcery.
This description, utilizing some pictographs partially produced by Sitting Bull in another context (Vestal, 1957), together with an artist's rendering of the central figures, has been used to create a visual image of this interesting robe (Fig. 4). (See also Taylor 1998).

Bild dieser interessanten Robe zu rekonstruieren (Abb. 4). (Siehe auch Taylor 1998.)

Sitting Bulls Kontakt mit katholischen Missionaren

Dass Sitting Bull überhaupt von der Existenz des Papstes wusste, ganz zu schweigen davon, dass er eine Robe als Geschenk für Seine Heiligkeit bemalte, wurde auf der Lund-Konferenz (1999) in Frage gestellt. Die zur Zeit vorhandenen Informationen belegen jedoch, dass Sitting Bull sehr wohl über den Römischen Katholizismus Bescheid wusste, dessen Kraftquelle, wie Smith es ausdrückte, *"irgendein Papst in Rom darstellte, offensichtlich ein anderer grosser Religionsführer, wie er selbst"* (Smith 1943: 197).

Sitting Bulls erster eingehender Kontakt mit einem katholischen Missionar und mit katholischen Lehren begann mit dem Besuch von Father Pierre-Jean de Smet bei den Hunkpapa und Blackfeet Sioux am 19. Juni 1868. Das Dorf der Sioux mit etwa 600 Zelten war an den Ufern des Yellowstone River errichtet worden, wenige Meilen oberhalb der Mündung des Powder River. Die Oberhäuptlinge waren zu dieser Zeit Black Moon, Four Horns und Red Horn. Jedoch empfing Sitting Bull, der für seine Grosszügigkeit gegenüber Fremden und

Sitting Bull's Contact with Catholic Missionaries

That Sitting Bull even knew of the existence of the Pope, let alone created a robe as a gift for his Holiness, was questioned at the Lund conference. However, the information available to date strongly suggests that Sitting Bull was very much aware of Roman Catholicism, the fountainhead of whose power, as Smith put it – "lay in a certain Pope of Rome, evidently another great religious chieftain like himself" (Smith 1943:197).

Sitting Bull's first sustained encounter with a Catholic Missionary and Catholic teachings occurred with the visit of Father Pierre-Jean De Smet to the Hunkpapa and Blackfeet Sioux on 19th June 1868. The Sioux village, consisting of some 600 lodges, was pitched on the banks of the Yellowstone River a few miles above the mouth of the Powder River. The principal chiefs at this time were Black Moon, Four Horns and Red Horn. Sitting Bull, however, known for his generosity to strangers as well as to his own people, received De Smet in his tipi where De Smet stayed until his return to Fort Rice on the morning of 21st June (Utley 1993:79-81). De Smet had with him his "standard of peace" which evoked much discussion; this was a

> Deloria:
>
> t'at'ą́ka 'iyótąke 'Supreme Bull'
>
> t'at'ą́ka 'íyotake 'Bull Sits'
>
> t'at'ą́ka-'i`yotake 'He Sits as a Bull'
>
> Handbook (Colorado):
>
> thathą́ka iyótąke 'Supreme Bull'
>
> thathą́ka íyotake 'Bull is in the process of sitting down'
>
> thathą́ka?íyotake 'One who sits like a bull'
>
> Phonetics: 'Supreme Bull' t^{kh}ah-t^{kh}UHNKA ee-YO-tuhn-ke (e = pet)
>
> 'Bull sits' t^{kh}ah-t^{kh}UHNKA EE-yo-tah-ke (2 words)
>
> 'Sits like bull' t^{kh}ah-t^{kh}UHNKA-ee-yo-tah-ke (1 word)
>
> ("kh" somewhat like the "ch" of German Bach)

Figure 9 Deloria's spelling of Sitting Bull's name contrasted with the recently developed system relating to Lakota phonetics and adopted in the new Handbook of North American Indians (Vol. 17). The 'ą́' with the nasal hook used by Deloria has been retained but the raised comma in the 't' (i.e. t) has been replaced by 'h' to indicate a strong guttural sound. The nasal hooked 'a' has often been replaced by 'ah' or simply ' '. In turn the 'ah' has sometimes been rendered 'an'. These variations have caused considerable confusion in the spelling of Sitting Bull's name. The rendering shown here, differs slightly from Deloria's original. Whose typesetter used a mirror image of the raised comma instead of a single quote. It does not matter which end of the 'apostrophe' or 'comma' has the heavy dot; what is important is the direction of the curve. The source of both marks is the Greek writing system, which used the left half of a circle for a word that began with an 'h' sound and the right half for a word that began with a vowel withhout the 'h'. Illustration, courtesy David Rood, Department of Linguistics. University of Colorado, Denver.

Abb. 9 Die Buchstabierung von Sitting Bulls Namen durch Deloria unterscheidet sich von dem neuerlich entwickelten System bezüglich Lakota-Phonetik, das vom neuen Handbook of North American Indians (Vol. 17) übernommen wurde. Das 'a' mit dem Nasal-Haken, das von Deloria benutzt wurde, wurde beibehalten, aber das hochgestellte Komma im 't' (d. i. t) wurde durch ein 'h' ersetzt, um einen starken gutturalen Klang anzuzeigen. Das 'ą́' mit dem Nasal-Haken wurde oft durch 'ah' oder ein einfaches 'a' ersetzt. Anderseits wurde das 'ah' manchmal als 'an' übertragen. Diese Varianten haben für erhebliche Verwirrung bei der Buchstabierung von Sitting Bulls/Supreme Bulls Namen gesorgt. Die hier vorgestellte Übertragung unterscheidet sich ein wenig von Delorias Original. Dessen Schriftsetzer benutzte ein spiegelbildliches hochgestelltes Komma, statt eines einfaches Anführungszeichens. Es ist egal, an welchem Ende des 'Apostrophs' oder 'Kommas' sich der Punkt befindet, bedeutsam ist die Ausrichtung der Krümmung. Quelle beider Markierungen ist das griechische Schriftsystem, das die linke Hälfte eines Kreises für ein Wort benutzt, dessen Anfang wie ein 'H' klingt, und die rechte Hälfte für ein Wort, das mit einem Vokal ohne das 'H' beginnt. Abbildung mit Genehmigung von David Rood, Department of Linguistics. University of Colorado, Denver.

seinen eigenen Leuten bekannt war, De Smet in seinem Tipi. Hier wohnte De Smet bis zu seinem Aufbruch nach Fort Rice am Morgen des 21. Juni (Utley 1993: 79-81). De Smet führte seine "Friedensflagge" mit sich, die eine lange Diskussion auslöste. Es handelte sich um ein Banner mit einem Bild der Jungfrau Maria, umgeben von goldenen Sternen (ibid: 79). Am Abend vor seinem Aufbruch erzählte De Smet Geschichten aus der Bibel, und es gab sicherlich einen Austausch von Gedanken über religiöse Überzeugungen. Sitting Bulls Onkel, Four Horns, eröffnete das Council mit einer umfangreichen Pfeifenzeremonie und De Smet mit einem kurzen Gebet. Während seines Aufenthalts segnete De Smet ferner eine Anzahl Kinder und taufte mehrere Männer.

In den folgenden zehn Jahren geriet Sitting Bull zunehmend in Kontakt mit verschiedenen Missionaren, wobei jeder ihn mit seinen besonderen Lehren bedrängte und zweifellos versuchte, ihn zu der jeweiligen religiösen Richtung zu bekehren. Der Tradition von De Smet folgte der Reverend Abbott Martin Marty, der insbesondere in den katholischen Missionen auf mehreren Missouri-River-Reservationen aktiv war (Manzione 1991: 48). Wie bereits im Haupttext erwähnt, erreichte Father Marty

banner which displayed an image of the Virgin Mary surrounded by gilt stars (ibid: 79). The evening before departure De Smet told stories from the Bible and there was clearly an exchange of ideas on religious beliefs. Thus, Sitting Bull's uncle, Four Horns, opened the council proceedings with an elaborate pipe ceremonial and De Smet with a short prayer. During his stay De Smet also blessed a number of children and baptized several men. Over the next decade, Sitting Bull would increasingly come into contact with various missionaries each exposing him to their particular beliefs, clearly in an attempt to convert him to their own brand of religion. Following in the tradition established by De Smet, was the Reverend Abbott Martin Marty who was particularly active at the Catholic missions on a number of the Missouri River Reservations (Manzione 1991:48). As has already been mentioned in the main text of this paper Father Marty arrived at Sitting Bull's camp in Wood Mountain in May 1877. Later, at Fort Peck, Montana, he reported on his visit stating that he was "received with great ceremony on Sunday morning 27th May".[21] A few days later on the morning of 2nd June a "great council was held" (Marquette Archives. B.C.I.M. Series I. Box 4 Folder 1) and later at the opening

Sitting Bulls Lager in Wood Mountain im Mai 1877. Später, in Fort Peck, Montana, berichtete er, dass er "mit einer grossen Zeremonie am Sonntagmorgen, dem 27. Mai" empfangen wurde.[21] Wenige Tage später, am Morgen des 2. Juni, wurde "ein grosses Council abgehalten" (Marquette Archives, B.C.I.M. Series 1. Box 4. Folder 1), und danach, bei der Eröffnungssitzung am Nachmittag, "lauschten" die Teilnehmer "einem Gebet von Pretty Bear, einem Hunkpapa, der Katholik war" (Manzione 1991: 49). Dass Father Marty letztlich bemüht war, Sitting Bull zum Katholizismus zu bekehren, geht aus einem Brief hervor, den er von der Standing Rock Agentur im August 1882 schrieb. In diesem Brief erwähnt Marty Sitting Bulls Gefangenschaft in Fort Randall und seine Bemühungen, ihn dorthin zurückzubringen, "wohin er gehört" (das heisst in die Standing Rock Reservation). Er war jedoch erpicht darauf, bis zum nächsten Frühling bei Sitting Bull in Fort Randall zu bleiben, äusserst besorgt darum, ihn "vor den Episkopalen zu retten". Er hoffte, die Hilfe eines einflussreichen Katholiken, des Abgeordneten Doucet, bei seinen Bemühungen zu gewinnen, Sitting Bull nach Hause zu bringen (Marquette Archives, B.C.I.M. Series I. Box 5. Folder 4). Später, Mitte der 1880er Jahre, nach session in the afternoon, the participants "listened to a prayer by Pretty Bear, a Hunkpapa who was a Catholic" (Manzione 1991:49). That Father Marty was subsequently intent on getting Sitting Bull's conversion to Catholicism, is indicated by a letter which he wrote from Standing Rock Agency in August 1882. In his letter, Marty makes reference to Sitting Bull's captivity at Fort Randall and the efforts which he had made to get him back to "where he belongs" (i.e. the Standing Rock Reservation). He was, however, keen to be with Sitting Bull at Fort Randall until the following spring and expresses concern about "saving him from the Episcopalians". He hoped to evoke the help of an influential Catholic, Representative Doucet, in the effort to get Sitting Bull home. (Marquette Archives. B.C.I.M. Series I. Box 5. Folder 4). Later, in the mid-1880s, after his return to the Standing Rock Reservation, Sitting Bull was to have considerable discourse, and later some dispute, with Father Francis M. Craft, a Catholic missionary, who was deeply influenced by Pope Léon XIII's efforts to foster American vocations. Sitting Bull's disagreement with Father Craft concerned a Hunkpapa Lakota woman *Pte-sanwanya-kapiwin* – "White Buffalo Woman". This

seiner Rückkehr auf die Standing Rock Reservation, führte Sitting Bull lange Gespräche und hatte dann einige Auseinandersetzungen mit Father Francis M. Craft, einem katholischen Missionar, der stark von den Bemühungen Papst Leos XIII. beeinflusst war, die amerikanischen Missionen zu pflegen. Sitting Bulls Streit mit Father Craft entstand wegen einer Hunkpapa-Lakota-Frau, *Pte-sanwanya-kapiwin* - "White Buffalo Woman". Dieser jungen Frau war wegen ihrer angeblich übernatürlichen Kräfte von ihrem Stamm ein sakraler Name verliehen worden. Father Craft, der sie offensichtlich zum Katholizismus überredete, rekrutierte sie später für die "Congregation of American Sisters". Crafts Gebaren verärgerte Sitting Bull offenbar, und er beschwerte sich beim Bureau of Indian Affairs.[22] Es gibt somit kaum Zweifel, dass Sitting Bull mit den Lehren des Katholizismus sowie der Ansicht der Katholiken über den Repräsentanten Gottes auf Erden vertraut war.[23] Es scheint, dass Sitting Bull, seit er Mitte dreissig war, bis zu seinem Tod von Katholiken "umgeben" war!

young woman had been given a sacred name by her tribe because of the unusual powers which she was said to display. Father Craft, who obviously influenced her to adopt Catholicism, later recruited her to the "Congregation of American Sisters". Craft's activities apparently did not please Sitting Bull and he lodged a complaint with the Bureau of Indian Affairs.[22]
There can thus be little doubt that Sitting Bull was well acquainted with the teachings of Catholicism together with the view held by the Catholics of the representative of God on earth.[23] Sitting Bull it seems, from his mid-thirties to the time of his death, was "surrounded" by Catholics!

Der Erwerb einer bemalten Robe und ihr Transfer nach Europa

Im Dezember 1884 schrieb Marty - jetzt Bischof von Dakota - an Father Craft und teilte ihm mit, dass er beabsichtige, "unmittelbar nach Ostern nach Rom zu reisen". Er drückte seine Hoffnung aus, dem Heiligen Vater berichten zu können, dass Sitting Bull zum Katholizismus konvertiert sei, und er erwähnte den eindrucksvollen Empfang, den Sitting Bull ihm 7 Jahre zuvor am Frenchman's Creek bereitet hatte. (Siehe weiter vorn in dieser Studie.) Marty wies Craft darauf hin, dass Sitting Bull möglicherweise "eine Bisonrobe anfertigen" würde, die das Treffen am Frenchman's Creek dokumentierte und die er (Marty) mit zu Papst Leo XIII. nehmen konnte.[24] Martys Biograph (Karolevitz 1980: 95) erwähnt die Tatsache, dass Marty in der Tat im April 1885 eine grosse bemalte Bisonrobe mit nach Rom nahm und persönlich dem Papst überreichte. Ob es sich um dieselbe Robe handelte, die in Paris ausgestellt und bis ins Detail von R. De Sémallé (weiter vorn in diesem Anhang) beschrieben wurde, lässt sich in diesem Stadium der Nachforschung nicht beantworten. Wie beschrieben, zeigt sie einige Szenen

Acquisition of a Painted Robe and Transfer to Europe

In December 1884 Marty, now Bishop of Dakota, wrote to Father Craft telling him that he intended to "go to Rome immediately after Easter". He expressed the hope that he would be able to report to the Holy Father that Sitting Bull had been converted to Catholicism and he made reference to the impressive reception which Sitting Bull had given him at Frenchman's Creek seven years previously (referred to earlier in this paper). Marty suggested to Craft that possibly Sitting Bull would "prepare a buffalo robe" which would document the Frenchman's Creek meeting and that he (Marty) could then take it along to Pope Léon XIII.[24]

Marty's biographer (Karolevitz 1980:95) makes reference to the fact that Marty did indeed take a large painted buffalo robe to Rome in April 1885 and personally delivered it to the Pope. Whether this was the same robe which was put on display in Paris and described in considerable detail by R. De Sémallé (earlier in this Appendix) is, at this stage of research, unresolved. It is described as showing some scenes of "Custer's Last Stand"; no reference is made to the cross-and-calumet-holding central

von Custers letzter Schlacht. Es gibt keinen Hinweis auf die Mittelfiguren mit Kreuz und Calumet, die höchst bedeutende Darstellungen der Piktographien waren. Somit zeigen beide Beschreibungen, wenn eine auch sehr kurz ist, keine eindeutige Verbindung.[25] (Es ist allerdings kaum anzunehmen, dass es zwei Roben gegeben haben soll!) Eine weitere eindeutige Erwähnung der Robe, die in Paris ausgestellt und von De Sémallé beschrieben wurde, stammt vom Gründer des Trocadero Museum, Paris, E. T. Hamy, der 1897 bemerkte: *"Etwa vor 11 Jahren konnte man eine herrliche Robe in Paris sehen, brandneu, die gerade von den Pieds Noirs angefertigt worden war und die Monsignore Martin Merry (sic) von dem angesehenen Häuptling Sitting Bull zu Papst Leo XIII. brachte"* (Hamy 1897). Hamys Erwähnung der "Blackfeet" deutet darauf hin, dass er zusätzliche Informationen gehabt haben könnte. Sitting Bull war Hunkpapa, aber die Blackfeet-Sioux waren sehr enge Verbündete, und es gab zahlreiche Heiraten innerhalb beider Gruppen. Trotz ausgiebiger Suche in den europäischen Sammlungen, um die "Papst-Robe" zu lokalisieren, wurde sie bisher nicht gefunden; sie könnte noch auftauchen (Taylor 1998: 37). Inzwischen kann Abb. 4 als ungefähre Rekonstruktion

figures which were the most important features of the pictographs. Thus, the two descriptions, albeit one very brief, do not clearly relate[25] (although it is difficult to accept that there were two robes!) A further clear reference to the robe which was put on display in Paris and described by De Sémallé, was made by the founder of the Trocadero Museum (Paris), E.T. Hamy, who observed in 1897 "One could still see in Paris, about 11 years ago a superb robe, brand new, which had just been made by, the Pieds Noirs and which Monsgr Martin Merry [sic] brought to Pope Léon XIII from the celebrated chief Sitting Bull." (Hamy 1897). Hamy's reference to "Blackfeet" suggests additional information may have been available to him. Sitting Bull was Hunkpapa but the Blackfeet Sioux were very closely allied and there was considerable intermarriage between the two groups. Although extensive searches have been made of the collections in Europe in an effort to locate the "Pope" robe, it has yet to be found; it may still resurface (Taylor 1998:37). In the meantime Fig. 4 must suffice as an approximate reconstruction. As indicated, this is based on De Sémallé's description. The particular reference to "Sitting Bull armed as usual with a lance" is significa nt since, according to

dienen. Wie erwähnt, basiert die Skizze auf De Sémallés Beschreibung. Der besondere Hinweis, "Sitting Bull, bewaffnet wie üblich mit einer Lanze" ist bedeutsam, weil - White Bull zufolge, einem Neffen Sitting Bulls - Sitting Bull die Lanze allen anderen Waffen vorzog.[26] Die Bemerkung von Hamy 1886, die Robe sei "brandneu", weist offensichtlich darauf hin, dass sie erst kurz vorher gefertigt wurde (was mit Martys Brief an Craft 1884 übereinstimmt).
Die Behauptung von De Sémallés, dass die Robe der Beleg für Sitting Bulls Konvertierung zum Katholizismus sei, ist jedoch zweifelhaft. Obwohl Sitting Bull an den religiösen Konzepten des weissen Mannes interessiert war, gibt es grundlegende Beweise, dass er nicht zum Katholizismus oder irgend einem anderen fremden Glauben konvertierte. Wahrscheinlicher ist, dass die prominente Darstellung von Kreuz und Calumet im Mittelpunkt der Robe ein Hinweis auf Symbole von gleicher religiöser Bedeutung in beiden Kulturen war - Empfindungen, die von religiösen Führern wie Sitting Bull zweifellos anerkannt wurden.
Vielleicht zeigte die Robe auch statt Father Marty und Sitting Bull (wie De Sémallé berichtete) tatsächlich das Bild eines berühmteren Missionars - Father Pierre-Jean De Smet -

White Bull one of Sitting Bull's nephews, he, Sitting Bull favoured the lance above all other weapons.[26] The reference by Hamy to the robe being "brand new" in 1886 obviously suggests a very recently produced article (consistent with Marty's letter to Craft in 1884). The report by De Sémallé that it shows Sitting Bull's conversion to Catholicism is, however, questionable. Although Sitting Bull was interested in the white man's religious concepts, the evidence is substantial that he was not converted to Catholicism or any other alien faith.
More probable is that the prominent depiction of cross and calumet at the centre of the robe make a reference to symbols of equal religious importance in the two cultures – sentiments which would be clearly recognised by such religious leaders as Sitting Bull.
Perhaps too, rather than the robe actually showing Father Marty and Sitting Bull (as De Sémallé recorded), it may in fact be a depiction of a more famous missionary – Father Pierre-Jean De Smet – and relating to the 1868 meeting when, as mentioned previously, both Four Horns (Sitting Bull's uncle) and Sitting Bull performed the pipe ceremonial whilst De Smet evoked the power of the cross.

und bezog sich auf das Treffen von 1868, als - wie vorher erwähnt - Four Horns (Sitting Bulls Onkel) und Sitting Bull das grosse Pfeifenzeremoniell durchführten, während De Smet die Macht des Kreuzes beschwor.

Kaum Zweifel können daran bestehen, dass die Robe existierte und nach Europa gelangt ist. Falls sie nicht von Sitting Bull bemalt, sondern von jemand anderem gefertigt worden sein sollte, werden natürlich mehrere weitere Fragen aufgeworfen. Nicht zuletzt nach den Motiven der führenden Persönlichkeiten, einen solchen Transfer - zumindest nach Paris - vorzunehmen. Und nach der Behauptung, dass der grosse religiöse Führer der Lakota, Sitting Bull, zum Katholiken geworden sei! Es wird interessant sein zu sehen, wie "der Fall" sich letztlich entwickelt.

That the robe existed and came to Europe there can be little doubt. If it was not painted by Sitting Bull but fabricated by another party then, of course several further questions arise, not least the motivations of the principal individuals involved in its transfer (at least) to Paris and the story that the great religious leader of the Lakotas, Sitting Bull, had become a Catholic!

It will be interesting to see how "the case" subsequently unfolds.

Fussnoten

1 (a) Hodge (ed.), 1907: 883.
(b) Ausführliche Quellen bezüglich der frühen Missionare in Nordamerika werden in ibid: 874 - 909 behandelt. Diese Studie von James Mooney ist wahrscheinlich eine der grundlegendsten und genauesten Betrachtungen über das Missionswesen von Katholiken, Baptisten, Methodisten, Jesuiten, Congretionalisten, Presbyterianern, Episcopalisten, Lutheranern, Quäkern, Moravian-Protestanten und Mormonen in Nordamerika, beginnend mit den spanischen Franziskanermönchen 1542. Nicht jeder wird jedoch seiner Schlussfolgerung zustimmen: "Die Missionare kämpften einen guten Kampf. Wo sie keine grossen Erfolge erzielten, liegt der Grund im unbezähmbaren Eigennutz des weissen Mannes oder in der angeborenen Inkompetenz und Unwürdigkeit der Menschen, für die sie arbeiten" (ibid: 908). Neueren Datums ist eine Serie von Essays über religiöse Zusammenhänge mit einer Betonung des Katholizismus, die im neuen Handbook of North American Indians publiziert wurde (Washburn (ed.), 1988, Vol. 4: 430 - 521), auf die der interessierte Leser hingewiesen wird.
2 Zwecks weiterer Erörterung dieser Angelegenheiten siehe Taylor, 1994 (a): 57 - 71.
3 (a) Siehe Agent, 1992: 7.
(b) Bailey, 1995: 10 - 26. In seiner Erörterung bezüglich der "grossen, geheimnisvollen Macht, die alles Leben beseelt", beobachtete La Flesche: "Es ist jedoch wahr, dass die Eingeborenen dieses Landes sich lange, bevor Europäer ihren Fuss auf diese Scholle gesetzt haben, viele Gedanken über diese Thematik gemacht und ihre Vorstellungen darüber formuliert haben" (ibid: 12).
4 (a) Es ist belegt, dass Sitting Bull als Junge tatsächlich von seinem Vater den Namen "Springender Dachs" erhielt. Da er ungewöhnliche Eigenarten zeigte - er war auf seine Weise starrsinnig und bedächtig - verdiente er sich den Namen *Huŋkeśni* oder "Langsam" (Utley 1993: 6).
(b) Buechel (1983) überträgt dieses Wort als Huhkesni, das er abwechselnd als "kraftlos" (S. 691) und "langsam" (S. 768) übersetzt. Die Bezeichnung "kraftlos" scheint unangemessen für den jungen Sitting Bull, da dieser tatsächlich von jedem Biographen als energischer, talentierter junger Mann beschrieben wird. Ein angesehener Biograph Sitting Bulls stellte fest: "Slow war ein starker, lebhafter junger Bursche und fand diese Welt sehr nach seinem Geschmack" (Vestal, 1957: 4). Während einer Adoptionszeremonie für den verstorbenen E. H. Blackmore in Fort Yates im Sommer 1964 erhielt Blackmore den Jungennamen von Sitting Bull - *Hunkeshnee*. Bezüglich der Frage nach seiner Bedeutung berichtet Blackmore: "In der Sprache der Sioux bedeutet dieser Name 'langsam', 'bedächtig' oder 'nachdenklich'. Sie sagten, sogar als er noch ziemlich jung war, war Sitting Bull bedächtig und nachdenklich in allem, was er tat" (Blackmore, 1988: 56).
Derartige Hinweise auf diese Seite von Sitting Bulls Charakter tauchen in Berichten von Personen auf, die Sitting Bull persönlich kannten oder eng mit seinem Leben und seiner Zeit verbunden waren. So berichtete Edwin H. Allison 1897 über eine ungewöhnliche Unterhaltung, die er mit Sitting Bull hatte. Das Gespräch bezog sich auf den Namen, den die Sioux Allison verliehen hatten - *Hoga* = "Fisch" - der anscheinend alte Sioux-Prophezeiungen berührte. Der gesamte Ton der Unterhaltung belegt eine sehr sorgfältige Überlegung Sitting Bulls in der Abwägung der Argumente, die Allison vorbrachte. Als Allison einmal dachte, das diskutierte Thema sei abgeschlossen, "weil Sitting Bull wieder für lange Zeit schwieg und ich annahm, er würde nichts mehr über dieses Thema sagen, kehrte er schliesslich dazu zurück." Edwin Allison hielt sich im Winter 1880-81 mit Sitting Bull in Kanada auf, zu der Zeit, als Verhandlungen über die Rückkehr der geflüchteten Sioux in die USA im Gang waren. In späteren Jahren war Allison Angestellter des Bureau of American Ethnologie, das seine Kenntnisse nutzte, indianische (Sioux?) Berichte zu übersetzen. (Siehe The Evening Star, 4. September 1897 und The Evening News (?), Washington, 3. Juli 1897.)
5 Vestal überträgt diesen Namen als *"Tatan´ka Iyota´ke, Tatan´ka Psi´ca, Tatan´ka Winju´ha Najin, Tatán´ka Wanji´la"* (Vestal 1957: 16). David Rood teilte mir mit, dass seine Lakota-Informanten

Footnotes

1. (a) Hodge (ed.), 1907:883.
   (b) Extensive references on the early missionaries in North America are dealt with in ibid:874-909. This paper by James Mooney, is probably one of the most authoritative and concise surveys relating to Catholic, Baptist, Methodist, Jesuit, Congregational, Presbyterian, Episcopalian, Lutheran, Friends of Quakers, Moravian Protestant and Mormon missionaries in North America, starting with the Spanish Franciscan Fathers in 1542. Not all, however, will agree with his concluding remarks: '...the missionaries have fought a good fight. Where they have failed to accomplish large results the reason lies in the irrepressible selfishness of the white man or in the innate incompetence and unworthiness of the people for whom they labored'(ibid:908). More recently, a series of essays relating to Religious Relations, with an emphasis on Catholicism, have been published in the new Handbook of North American Indians (Washburn (ed.), 1988:Vol.4:430-521), to which the interested reader is referred.
2. For a further discussion of these issues, see Taylor, 1994 (a):57-71).
3. (a) See Agent, 1992:7.
   (b) Bailey, 1995:10-26. In his discussion relating to 'the great, mysterious Power that animates all life', La Flesche observed: 'It is true, however, that the natives of this land had given these themes much thought and had formulated their ideas concerning them long before the European set foot upon this soil' (ibid:12).
4. (a) The evidence is that Sitting Bull's actual boyhood name, given to him by his father, was Jumping Badger. Because he displayed unusual characteristics, being wilful and deliberate in his ways, he earned the name *Huŋkeśni*, or 'Slow' (Utley, 1993:6).
   (b) Buechel (1983) renders this word as Huhkesni, which he translates variously as 'feeble' (p.699), and 'slow' (p.768). The appellation 'feeble' seems inappropriate for the young Sitting Bull, since virtually every biographer refers to him as a vigorous and able young man. One respected biographer of Sitting Bull observed: ' 'Slow' was a strong, lively lad, and found this world greatly to his liking' (Vestal, 1957:4). At an adoption ceremonial of the late E.H. Blackmore, which took place at Fort Yates in the summer of 1964, Blackmore gave the boyhood name of Sitting Bull – *Hunkeshnee*. On enquiring as to its meaning, Blackmore reports: 'In the Sioux language this name meant 'slow', 'deliberate' or 'thoughtful'. They said even when he was quite young Sitting Bull was deliberate and thoughtful in everything he did' (Blackmore, 1988:56).
   Such sentiments relating to this side of Sitting Bull's character, have come down in reports relating to those who knew Sitting Bull personally or were closely in contact with his life and times. Thus, in 1897, Edwin H. Allison reported on an unusual conversation which he had with Sitting Bull. The conversation related to Allison's name which the Sioux had given him – *Hoga*, 'Fish', which it appeared touched on some ancient Sioux prophecy. The whole tone of conversation indicates a very careful deliberation on the part of Sitting Bull in weighing up the facts presented by Allison. At one stage, Allison thought that the topic under discussion was finished, since Sitting Bull 'was silent again for a long time, and I began to think that he would say nothing further on the subject, but at last he [returned to it]'. Edwin Allison stayed with Sitting Bull in Canada during the winter of 1880-81, at the time negotiations were taking place relating to the refugee Sioux returning to the United States. In later years, Allison was employed by the Bureau of American Ethnology, using his expertise in translating Indian (Sioux?) records. (See The Evening Star, September 4, 1897 and the Evening News (?), Washington, July 3, 1897).
5) Vestal renders these names as *'Tatan´ka Iyota´ke, Tatan´ka Psi´ca, Tatan´ka Winju´ha Najin, Tatán´ka Wanji´la'* respectively (Vestal, 1957:16). David Rood informs me that his Lakota informants, 'as the back-translation from English' gave *'T'at'ą́ka-'Iyotake'* for the first name. Using the nomenclature adopted in the Handbook of North American Indians (Vol. 17), this would be

"als Rückübersetzung aus dem Englischen" *"T'at'ą́ka-'Iyotake"* als Vornamen angeben. Der Nomenklatura des Handbook of North American Indians zufolge (Vol. 17), müsste dies *"Thatą́ka?iyotake"* geschrieben werden, "Einer, der wie ein Bisonbulle sitzt" (DR and CFT, 10. Juni 1999. (Siehe auch Anhang I.)

6 Für eine detaillierte Erörterung des Cheyenne-Kosmos und verwandter religiöser Konzepte siehe Moore (1974), insbesondere S. 145-166, und neueren Datums, Nagy (1994), der speziell bezüglich des Blauen Himmels und des Alls als Lebensspender auf Mutter Erde eine einfühlsame Erklärung liefert.

7 (a) Eine Darlegung des *Tobtob* kin findet sich in DeMallie und Lavenda (1977), die sich ferner auf die Pionierarbeit J. R. Walkers beziehen.

(b) Siehe auch Taylor (1989, 1994 (a) und 1994 (b) bezüglich einer Diskussion über religiöse Konzepte der Siouan.

8 Siehe Boas und Deloria (1939: 70). Diese Autoren weisen nachdrücklich auf die Fehler hin, die bei der Übersetzung von Eigennamen ins Englische auftreten können, speziell auf die Bedeutung des im Namen verwendeten Hauptworts und Verbums. Rood wies auf die Bedeutung der Hervorhebung von Buchstaben hin (DR an CFT, 8. Juni 1999). Wie Dahlstrom darlegt, bedeuten Schwächen, die ein Lakota-Sprecher auf dieser Ebene linguistischer Analyse zeigt "Zweifel am Wert einer umfassenden Schlussfolgerung" (Dahlstrom, 1987: 1.009).

9 (a) Angeblich berichtete Father De Smet, dass er, als er Sitting Bull traf, das Gefühl hatte, sich in Gesellschaft eines ungewöhnlichen Mannes zu befinden. (Bemerkung von Laura Peers auf dem 20. American Indian Workshop, Lund, Schweden, April 1999).

(b) Das Kruzifix aus Messing und Holz "blieb lange ein wertvoller Besitz der Sitting Bull-Familie" (Vestal 1957: 109). Vestal berichtete 1932, dass es sich zu dieser Zeit in seinem Besitz befände. Bezüglich detaillierterer Erörterungen der "Sitting Bull-Kruzifixe" sei der interessierte Leser auf Hollow (1984) und Hollow und Hoover (1984) verwiesen.

10 Siehe Diessner, 1993: 82, der diese Episoden in eine interessante erzählende Form bringt. Die damaligen Unterhaltungen zwischen Marty, Irvine und Sitting Bull sind gut dokumentiert in Manzione, 1991; siehe insbesondere S. 47 - 51.

11 Indem man Sitting Bull nahezu zwei Jahre in Gefangenschaft in Fort Randall festhielt, wurde es einem starken Indianeragenten ermöglicht, sich auf der Standing Rock Reservation zu etablieren. Dieser Agent war James McLaughlin, der im September 1881 Fort Yates erreichte, um die Leitung der Agentur von Standing Rock zu übernehmen (Diessner 1993: 97).

12 Ahern berichtete später, dass er Sitting Bull als "sehr bemerkenswerten Mann erlebte,... mit dem Auftreten eines Menschen, der seiner selbst bewusst war... Ich stand mehrere Monate lang in täglichem Kontakt mit Sitting Bull, und meine Bewunderung für ihn und seine vielen guten Eigenschaften wuchs." Ahern, ein ausgewiesener Linguist, der Französisch und Deutsch ebenso beherrschte wie Lakota, übersetzte die Briefe, die von Verehrern aus Frankreich und Deutschland eintrafen (Diessner 1993: 148). Viele Jahre später war seine offensichtliche Hochachtung für Sitting Bull ungebrochen als er, jetzt pensioniert aber noch immer aus dem Kriegsministerium in Washington D. C. schreibend (20. Juni 1929) eine Einladung zum Lunch mit Red Tomahawk ablehnte. Er erwähnte den Schock und sein Entsetzen, als er von Sitting Bulls Tod hörte. Ferner beobachtete er - offenbar in Würdigung seines einstigen Schützlings -, dass "Indianerhäuptlinge aus dem gesamten Sioux-Territorium kamen und seinen Rat suchten. Ich wurde stets von Sitting Bull gebeten, diesen Konferenzen beizuwohnen und fand sie höchst interessant, da sie den tiefen Respekt zeigten, der Sitting Bull von seinem Volk gezollt wurde" (ibid.).

13 Vestal berichtet, dass Sitting Bull "ein eifriger Beobachter von Vögeln und ihres Verhaltens" war und dass er gern "Geschichten über das Vogelvolk erzählte". Angeblich lernte er, die Sprache der Vögel zu verstehen, insbesondere der Elster und der westlichen Wiesenlerche; letzterer Vogel "sprach so gut Sioux, dass er auch als Sioux-Vogel bekannt ist" (Vestal 1957: 21). Utley berichtete,

written as *Tȟatȟą́ka?iyotake*, 'One who sits like a bull' (DR to CFT, 10 June, 1999). (See, however, Appendix I).
6   For a detailed discussion of the Cheyenne cosmos and related religious concepts, see Moore (1974), particularly pp. 145-166 and more recently, Nagy (1994) who, in particular, gives an insightful rendering relating to the Blue Sky – Space engendering life on Mother Earth (Fig. 5: p. 42).
7   (a) A discussion of the *Tobtob* kin is in DeMallie and Lavenda (1977) who also draw on the pioneer work of J. R. Walker.
    (b) See also Taylor (1989, 1994(a) and 1994(b)) for a discussion of Siouan religious concepts.
8   See Boas and Deloria (1939:70). These authors clearly indicate the errors which can occur in the translation into English of proper names and the importance of recognizing the nominalized noun and verb. Recently, Rood (DR to CFT, 8 June, 1999), pointed out the importance of the aspiration on letters. As Dahlstrom indicates, weaknesses displayed by a Lakota speaker at this level of linguistic analyses, will "call into question the validity of the larger conclusions" which such individuals may draw (Dahlstrom, 1987:1009).
9   (a) Father De Smet is said to have reported that when he met Sitting Bull he felt he was in the presence of an unusual man. (Comment from Laura Peers, 20th American Indian Workshop, Lund, Sweden. April 1999).
    (b) The crucifix of brass and wood, 'long remained a treasured possession' in the Sitting Bull family (Vestal, 1957:109). Vestal reported in 1932, that it was then in his possession. For a more detailed discussion of the 'Sitting Bull crucifixes', the interested reader is referred to Hollow (1984) and Hollow and Hoover (1984).
10 See Diessner, 1993:82, who puts these episodes in an interesting narrative form. The conversations between Marty, Irvine and Sitting Bull at this time, are well documented in Manzione, 1991: see particularly pp. 47-51.
11 This, almost two year confinement at Fort Randall was possibly contrived to enable a strong Indian agent to establish himself on the Standing Rock Reservation. The agent was James McLaughlin, who arrived at Fort Yates in September 1881, to take charge as the agent for Standing Rock Reservation (Diessner, 1993:97).
12 Ahern later reported that he found Sitting Bull, a 'very remarkable man...[with] manner of a man who knew his ground....For several months I was in daily contact with Sitting Bull, and learned to admire him for his many fine qualities'. Ahern, an accomplished linguist, who spoke French and German as well as Lakota, translated the letters which came from admirers in France and Germany (Diessner, 1993:148). Many years later, it was obvious that the high regard in which he held Sitting Bull, had not waned when, now retired but writing from the War Department in Washington, D.C. (20 June, 1929), he declined an invitation to have lunch with Red Tomahawk. He reported on his shock and dismay when he heard of Sitting Bull's death. He further observed – obviously as a tribute to his old charge – 'Indian chiefs from all over the Sioux Territory came to seek his advice. I was always asked by Sitting Bull to attend these conferences, and found them most interesting, as they showed the deep respect in which Sitting Bull was held by his people' (ibid.).
13 Vestal reports that Sitting Bull was 'a close student of birds and their ways' and that he was 'fond of telling stories about the Bird People'. It was said that he learned to understand the speech of birds, particularly the magpie and the Western meadowlark and that this latter bird spoke 'such good Sioux that it is known as the Sioux bird' (Vestal, 1957:21). Utley reported the Sioux recalled occasions on which Sitting Bull 'spoke to buffalo and wolves' (Utley, 1993:30). Little wonder he was regarded as an outstanding *Wichasha Wakan, [wicasa wakan],* 'Holy Man' (ibid:26).
14 The contract between Sitting Bull and Buffalo Bill's Wild West, signed by Sitting Bull and John M. Burke (An agent for William Cody) and witnessed by James McLaughlin on 6 June, 1885, paid Sitting Bull 50 dollars per week. He also had sole right to sell his own photographs and autograph

dass die Sioux sich an Gelegenheiten erinnerten, bei denen "Sitting Bull mit Bisons und Wölfen sprach" (Utley 1993: 30). Kein Wunder, dass er als aussergewöhnlicher *Wichasha Wakan [Wicasa wakan]*, als "Heiliger Mann" verehrt wurde (ibid: 26).

14 Der Vertrag zwischen Sitting Bull und Buffalo Bill's Wild West, unterschrieben von Sitting Bull und John M. Burke (einem Agenten William Codys) und bezeugt von James McLaughlin am 6. Juli 1885 sicherte Sitting Bull eine Bezahlung von wöchentlich 50 $. Ferner erhielt er das ausschliessliche Recht, seine Fotos und sein Autogramm zu verkaufen. (Eines davon wurde in unserer Zeit für 750 Pfund in einem Auktionshaus in Nottingham, England, verkauft. Siehe Daily Mail, London, 6. Dezember 1990.)
Der Originalvertrag, der von Burdick publiziert wurde (1941: 18-19) wurde kürzlich wiederentdeckt (Kortlander, 1997: 1 und 5-9) und wird jetzt im Custer Battlefield Museum in Garryowen, Montana, ausgestellt. Wie Kortlander feststellte, waren 50 $ wöchentlich im Jahr 1885 eine ausserordentliche Bezahlung. Er erwähnte jedoch, dass Sitting Bull nur wenig davon für sich selbst behielt. Er schickte "den grössten Teil seines Verdienstes ... an seine Frau und die Familie, die noch immer auf Standing Rock waren, und er beschenkte grosszügig arme Kinder - Zeitungsjungen, Schuhputzer und andere heimatlose Gassenjungen - die er auf den Strassen sah, während er mit der Show reiste" (ibid: 7 - 8). Sitting Bulls ausserordentliche Grosszügigkeit gegenüber seinem eigenen Volk war bekannt (Utley 1993: 27), eine Eigenschaft, die er offenbar auch auf weniger glückliche Mitglieder der weissen Rasse ausdehnte."

15 Zur ausführlichen Erörterung dieses Themas siehe Taylor, 1989.

16 Peterson und Peers zufolge wurde die Katholische Leiter durch Bischof Blanchet 1838 in Oregon eingeführt. Die Einführung war umstritten, weil sie die Protestanten in einer Sackgasse, die von der einzigen Strasse zur Erlösung abwich, darstellte. Die Protestanten entwarfen eine Darstellung mit ihrer eigenen Version, der "Protestantischen Leiter". Diese zeigte die Katholiken auf einem Irrweg und den Papst, der am Jüngsten Tag ins Höllenfeuer stürzt. (Offenbar verursachte diese "Kriegsführung" zwischen Katholiken und Protestanten Verwirrung unter den Indianern, die zum Christentum bekehrt werden sollten - siehe Peterson und Peers 1993: 111.) Die Leiter wurde von De Smet überarbeitet und 1843 in Paris gedruckt. Fast 30 Jahre später entwickelte Father Albert Lacombe, der viele Jahre bei kanadischen Plainsindianern zubrachte, eine Version der "Leiter", die als "biblische und kirchliche Geschichte in Bildern" beschrieben wurde. Es wird berichtet, dass Tausende von Exemplaren in Frankreich gedruckt wurden,und als sie Papst Pius IV gezeigt wurde, verlangte dieser, dass "viele Tausend Exemplare hergestellt werden sollten" (Hughes 1911: 203). John C. Ewers war der Meinung, dass die Idee einer "Himmelsleiter" zur Verbreitung des Christentums im 19. Jahrhundert auch weithin von anderen Glaubensgemeinschaften genutzt wurde (JCE an CFT, 3. Juli 1992).

17 Dies wurde von Dr. Cyril W. Grave berichtet, ehemals Superintendent der Schulen von Bullhead auf der Standing Rock Reservation (siehe Taylor, 1998: 11 und Fussnote 3).

18 Die genauen Umstände, unter denen Dr. Horace Deeble, der diensthabende Militärarzt von Fort Yates, sich diese Skalplocke aneignete, sind in Taylor (1998) dokumentiert, hier ist auch die Skalplocke abgebildet, Abb. 9.

19 Dies wird kurz erörtert in Taylor, Tyler (ed.) (1994a: 69). Siehe auch eine eingehende Darstellung der Ansicht der Plainsindianer bezüglich Medizinbündeln in Waugh (1990).

20 (a) The Independent Newspaper, 24. August 1992.
(b) Begley, 1998: 44 - 49.

21 Ein Bericht über diesen Besuch, wahrscheinlich von Father Marty verfasst, wurde im folgenden Jahr veröffentlicht. Danach "kam ihm Sitting Bull persönlich, an der Spitze von 100 berittenen Kriegern, entgegen und sang Lieder der Freude und des Willkommens". Er wurde zum Lager eskortiert und erhielt ein bequemes Zelt, und "alle Männer und Frauen kamen heran, um ihn zu begrüssen". Sitting Bull sagte dann zu ihm: "[Obwohl] du aus Amerika kommst ... bist du ein Priester und willkommen. Der Priester bedroht niemanden, und wir werden ihm Essen und Schutz

(one of these was recently sold for £750 at a Nottingham Auction House, England. See the Daily Mail, London, December 6, 1990). This original contract, which was published by Burdick (1941:18-19), has recently been rediscovered (Kortlander, 1997:1 and 5-9), and was on display in the Museum at the Garryowen Trading Post, Montana. As Kortlander observed, 50 dollars a week was exceptional pay for 1885; however, he further reports that Sitting Bull kept little of it for himself, sending the 'majority of his earnings…to his wife and family', who were still at Standing Rock and giving generously to the poor children – newsboys, bootblacks and other destitute street urchins – who he saw on the road whilst touring with the show (ibid:7-8). Sitting Bull was well known for his exceptional generosity amongst his own people (Utley, 1993:27), an attribute he was clearly inclined to extend to less fortunate members of the white race.
15 For more discussion on this subject, see Taylor, 1989).
16 According to Peterson and Peers, the Catholic Ladder was invented by Bishop Blanchet in Oregon in 1838. The invention was controversial since it showed the Protestants marooned on a dead end branch of the one time road to salvation. The Protestants counteracted this with their own version 'The Protestant Ladder'. This showed the Catholics on the wrong road and the Pope falling into the fires of hell on Judgement Day. (Obviously, this 'warfare' between the Catholics and Protestants, caused confusion with the Indians that they were trying to convert to Christianity – see Peterson and Peers, 1993:111). The Ladder was revised by De Smet and it was printed in Paris in 1843. Almost thirty years later, Father Albert Lacombe, who spent many years amongst the Canadian Plains Indians, developed a version of the *echelle* which was described as a 'Bible and Church history in pictures'. It is reported that thousands of copies of it were printed in France and that when Pope Pius IV was shown it, he requested that 'several thousand copies [be] made' (Hughes, 1911:203). John C. Ewers expressed the opinion that the idea of a 'ladder to heaven' in teaching about Christianity, was widely used by other denominations [in the nineteenth century] (JCE to CFT. July 3, 1992).
17 This was reported by Dr. Cyril W. Grace, formerly Superintendent of Schools at Bullhead on the Standing Rock Reservation (see Taylor, 1998:11 and note 3).
18 The full circumstances of the removal of this scalp-lock by Dr. Horace Deeble, Acting Assistant Post Surgeon at Fort Yates, is documented in Taylor (1998). A photograph of the scalp-lock is illustrated in that volume, Fig. 9.
19 This is briefly discussed in Taylor, Tyler ed., (1994a:69). See also a more detailed discussion of the Plains Indians' stance towards Medicine Bundles, in Waugh (1990).
20 (a) The Independent Newspaper, August 24th, 1992.
(b) Begley, 1998:44-49.
21 A report on this visit, presumably written by Father Marty, was published the following year. He recorded "Sitting Bull himself, at the head of one hundred mounted warriors, came out to meet him, singing songs of gladness and welcome". He was escorted to camp and assigned a comfortable tent and "all the men and women [came] forth to give him welcome". Sitting Bull then said to him "[Although] you come from America…. You are a priest and welcome. The priest harms no man, and we will give him food and protection and listen to his words".
Although Marty's description of his experience in the Sioux camp differs somewhat from the reports of the Canadian Mounted Police (Manzione 1991:46), his description of life in the village and references to Sitting Bull's obvious high status in both social and religious affairs, is highly perceptive and fascinating (Marquette Archives B.C.I.M. Series U2. Jan 1878).
22 Sitting Bull's obvious concerns about Craft may have been well founded. Although clearly sincere in his beliefs and spending about twenty years amongst the Sioux, the Catholic hierarchy in the United States apparently refused to support his missionary efforts. (I am indebted to Tom Foley of Dunwoody, Georgia for this information, who is at present writing a biography of Father Craft).
23 When Sioux Indians visited the Vatican with Buffalo Bill's Wild West in 1890 they apparently came

gewähren und seinen Worten lauschen." Obwohl Martys Beschreibung seiner Erlebnisse im Lager der Sioux sich etwas von den Berichten der Canadian Mounted Police unterscheidet (Manzione 1991: 46), ist seine Darstellung des Lebens im Dorf und der Verweis auf Sitting Bulls offensichtlich hohe Stellung in sozialen und religiösen Angelegenheiten höchst einfühlsam und faszinierend (Marquette Archives, B.C.I.M. Series U2. Jan. 1878).

22 Sitting Bull dürfte gute Gründe gehabt haben, wegen Craft besorgt zu sein. Obwohl er sehr ernsthaft in seinem Glauben war und etwa 20 Jahre unter den Sioux zugebracht hatte, verweigerte die katholische Hierarchie in den Vereinigten Staaten offenbar die Unterstützung seiner missionarischen Bemühungen. (Ich schulde Tom Foley aus Dunwoody, Georgia, Dank für seine Information. Mr. Foley schreibt z. Zt. eine Biographie über Father Craft.)

23 Als Sioux-Indianer mit Buffalo Bill's Wild West 1890 den Vatikan besuchten, kehrten sie offenbar etwas desillusioniert zurück. Nate Salisbury zufolge sagten die Indianer, dass sich einiges ändern müsse, "bevor sie irgendetwas von dem glauben würden, was die [katholischen] Missionare ihnen künftig erzählten" (Wilson und Martin 1998: 79).

24 Brief von Marty an Craft, 17. Dez. 1884. (Mit Genehmigung von Tom Foley. Siehe Fussnote 22.)

25 Schwester Duratschek erwähnt eine "schöne Bisonrobe, auf die ein Neffe Sitting Bulls indianische Szenen gemalt habe, darunter die tragische letzte Schlacht Custers" (Duratschek 1979: 97).

26 Sitting Bulls Lanze wird als 7 oder 8 Fuss lang beschrieben, mit einer 8 Inch langen eisernen Spitze. Sie wurde ihm zusammen mit einem Schild zur Zeit seines ersten Coups von seinem Vater geschenkt. Seine Mutter hatte sie mit Verzierungen aus blauen und weissen Perlen versehen. Die Perlen waren um die gesamte Länge des Schaftes gewickelt. Am Ende war eine einzelne Feder befestigt (Utley 1993: 19).'

away somewhat disillusioned. Nate Salisbury reported that the Indians, said things would have to change if they were to "believe anything the [Catholic] missionaries might tell them in future" (Wilson and Martin 1998:79)!

24 Letter from Marty to Craft, 17th December 1884. (Courtesy, Tom Foley. See note 22).
25 Sister Duratschek makes reference to "a handsome buffalo robe upon which a nephew of Sitting Bull had painted Indian scenes, among them the tragic Custer's last stand" (Duratschek 1979:97).
26 Sitting Bull's lance is described as being seven or eight feet long and tipped with an eight inch iron blade; it was, together with a shield, given to him by his father at the time of his first coup. It was embellished with blue and white beads which had been contributed by his mother. The beads were wrapped along the entire length of the shaft, to the end of which was attached a single feather (Utley 1993:19).

Bibliography/Bibliographie

Agent, Dan
1992   LaFlesche Papers Reveal Osage Intellect and Logic. Smithsonian Runner 92-4:7. Washington: Smithsonian Institution.

Allison, Edwin H.
1897   (a) Old Sitting Bull: His Story of the Massacre of General Custer's Army...Scout Allison Tells of the Great Sioux Prophet...The Evening Star, September 4.
(b) Scout Allison's Story... Evening News(?), July 3. Washington.

Balmer, Joseph
1975 and 1998/9 Personal communications to the author relating to Sitting Bull. June 1975/98/99. Zurich. In author's possession.

Begley, Sharon
1998   Science Finds God. Newsweek, July 27:44-49. New York.

Blackmore, Edward H.
1988   Hunkeshnee: The Memoirs of Ted Blackmore. Brighton: The Friends of Ted Blackmore.

Blish, Helen H.
1967   A Pictographic History of the Oglala Sioux. Lincoln. University of Nebraska Press.

Boas, Franz and Ella Deloria
1939   Dakota Grammar. Memoirs of the National Academy of Sciences 23 (Pt. 2). Washington: U.S. Government Printing Office.

Buechel, Rev. Eugene
1983   Lakota-English Dictionary. Pine Ridge, South Dakota: Red Cloud Indian School Inc.

Burdick, Usher L.
1941   The Last Days of Sitting Bull: Sioux Medicine Chief. Baltimore: Wirth Brothers.

Carriker, Robert C.
1995　　Father Peter John De Smet: Jesuit in The West. Norman. University of Oklahoma Press.

Dahlstrom, Amy
1987　　Review of Sacred Language: The Nature of Supernatural Discourse in Lakota (William K. Powers). American Anthropologist 89:4:1009.

Densmore, Frances
1918　　Teton Sioux Music. Washington; Bureau of American Ethnology, Bulletin 61. Smithsonian Institution.

DeMallie, Raymond J.,
and Robert H. Lavenda
1977　　Wakan: Plains Siouan Concepts of Power. The Anthropology of Power Raymond D. Fogelson and Richard Adams, eds. New York: Academic Press.

Diessner, Don
1993　　There Are No Indians Left But Me! SITTING BULL'S STORY. Great Native American Leaders Series. Vol. 1. El Segundo, California: Upton and Sons.

Duratschek, Mary C.
1979　　Builders of God's Kingdom: The history of the Catholic church in South Dakota. South Falls.

Ewers, John C.
1956　　The Gun of Sitting Bull. The Beaver, Magazine of the North, Outfit 287:20-23. Winnipeg: Hudson's Bay Co.

Feest, Christian et al
1999　　Sitting Bull: Der Letzte Indianer. Darmstadt. Landesmuseum.

Fiske, Frank Bennett
1933　　Life and Death of Sitting Bull. Fort Yates, North Dakota: Pioneer-Arrow print.

Foley, Tom
1999　　Communications with the author relating to the Sitting Bull/Pope robe. July. Dunwoody, Georgia.

Hamy, E.T.
1897 Robe Biographique en Peau de Bison d'un Guerrier Dakota. Vol. 1. Paris: Galerie Américaine du Trocadéro.

Hedren, Paul L.
1997 Sitting Bull's Surrender at Fort Buford. Williston, North Dakota: Fort Union Association.

Hodge, Frederick Webb, ed.
1907- Handbook of American Indians North of Mexico. 2 vols. Washington: Bureau of American Ethnology,
1910 Smithsonian Institution. (Reprinted: Rowman and Littlefield Inc., New York. 1965).

Hollow, Robert C.
1984 Sitting Bull: Artifact and Artifake. Address given at the 8th Annual Plains Indian Seminar, Buffalo Bill Historical Center, Cody, Wyoming. September 29.

Hollow, Robert C. and
Herbert T. Hoover
1984 The Last Years of Sitting Bull. Bismarck: State Historical Society of North Dakota.

Hughes, Katherine
1911 Father Lacombe: The Black-Robe Voyageur. New York: Moffat, Yard and Company.

Karolevitz, Robert F.
1980 Bishop Martin Marty: "The Black Robe Lean Chief". Yankton, South Dakota. Benedictine Sisters of Sacred Heart Convent.

Keller, Ruth and
Lohhausen, Hans
1989 Rudolf Cronau, Journalist und Künstler. Bergischer Geschichtsverein, Solingen.

Kortlander, Christopher
1997 The Showman, the Chief and the newly-found contract. The Indian Trader 28-4:1 and 5-9. Gallup.

La Flesche, Francis
1995   The Osage and the Invisible World: From The Works of Francis La Flesche. Garrick A. Bailey, ed. Vol. 217 in The Civilization of the American Indian Series. Norman and London: University of Oklahoma Press.

MacEwan, Grant
1973   Sitting Bull: The Years in Canada. Edmonton: Hurtig Publishers.

Manzione, Joseph
1991   I Am Looking to the North for My Life: Sitting Bull 1876-1881. Salt Lake City: University of Utah Press.

Marquis, Thomas B.
1934   Sitting Bull and Gall, the Warrior. Published by the author. Scottsdale: Cactus Pony.

Moore, John Hartwell
1974   A Study of Religious Symbolism among the Cheyenne Indians. Ph.D Thesis. New York University.

Nagy, Imre
1994   Cheyenne Shields and their Cosmological Background. American Indian Art 19-3: 38-47. Scottsdale.

Peterson, Jacqueline and
Laura Peers
1993   Sacred Encounters. The De Smet Project. Norman and London: Washington State University and University of Oklahoma Press.

Powers, William K.
1986   Sacred Language. Norman: University of Oklahoma Press.

Rood, David
1999   Personal communications to the author re (a) Sitting Bull/Supreme Bull in Lakota (b) The University of Colorado system of rendering Lakota (Lakhota). Koln and Denver, June/July 1999. In author's possession.

Rood, David S. and
Allan R. Taylor
1996   Sketch of Lakhota, a Siouan Language. Handbook of North American Indians. Ives Goddard, ed. Vol. 17:440-482. Washington: Smithsonian Institution.

Sémallé, R. de
1885   La robe de Sitting-Bull. Vol. IV:369. Revue d'Ethnographie.

Smith, DeCost
1943   Indian Experiences. Caldwell, Idaho: The Caxton Printers Ltd.

Taylor, Colin
1975   The Warriors of the Plains. London: Hamlyn Ltd.

1989   Wakanyan: Symbols of Power and Ritual of the Teton Sioux. Amerindian Cosmology. Cosmos 4:237-257; Yearbook of the Traditional Cosmology Society. Brandon, Manitoba: The Canadian Journal of Native Studies.

1994 (a) Taku Skanskan: Power Symbols of the Universe: parallels in the Cosmos of Plains Indians and White Missionaries. Suzanne G. Tyler, ed. The Artist & The Missionary. The Proceedings of the 1992 Plains Indian Seminar, Buffalo Bill Historical Center: 57-71. Wyoming: Cody.

1994 (b) The Plains Indians. London: Salamander Books, Ltd.

1996   Plains Indians and White Missionaries. The English Westeners Society. Special Publication No 8A. Barry C. Johnson & Francis B. Taunton (eds). London.

1998   Iho'lena: Voices from the past; messages for the future. Cultural, religious and military content of Plains Indian artefacts. (Bilingual: English-German). Wyk auf Foehr: Verlag fur Amerikanistik.

Utley, Robert M.
1993   The Lance and The Shield: The Life and Times of Sitting Bull. New York: Ballantine Books.

Vestal, Stanley

1957   Sitting Bull. Champion of the Sioux. Norman: University of Oklahoma Press.

Washburn, Wilcomb E., ed.
1988   Handbook of North American Indians: History of Indian-White Relations. Vol. 4. Washington: Smithsonian Institution.

Waugh, Earle H.
1990   Blackfoot Religion: My Clothes are Medicine. The Scriver Blackfoot Collection: Repatriation of Canada's Heritage. Philip H. R. Stepney and David J. Goa, eds. Edmonton: Provincial Museum of Alberta.

Wilson, R & Martin, G.
1998   Buffalo Bill's Wild West. London. Greenhill Books.

Cover/Titelbild - Frontiespiece/Frontispiz

Cover: A reconstruction of the central images on the robe said to have been sent to the Pope in Rome by T'at'ah'ka 'Iyo'tahke. The figures were described in some detail when the robe was put on display in Paris in 1884 (see AppendixII). Of this robe, Martin Marty recorded 'I go to Rome immediately after Easter, and would like to bring to the Holy Father the news that Sitting Bull is a member of the Church. He might prepare a buffalo robe, on which he could represent the reception they gave me in their camp on Frenchmen's Creek in May 1877. I would take it along to Leo XIII ...'. Although all evidence suggests that no conversion of the Hunkpapa leader to Catholicism occurred, Father Marty **did** get the robe and, according to Marty's biographer, the Bishop personally delivered it to Leo XIII in April 1885. However, the figures may make reference to the visit of Father Pierre-Jean De Smet to the Sioux village on the Powder River in June 1868 (see Fig. 1), when the meeting was opened with an elaborate pipe ceremonial. (Sketch by Peter Bowles).
(Author and publisher express their special thanks to the artist, Peter Bowles, for his permission to use this sketch as cover illustration for this study).

Titelbild: Eine Rekonstruktion des zentralen Motivs auf der Robe, die angeblich von T'at'ah'ka 'Iyo'tahke an den Papst in Rome gesandt wurde. Die Gestalten wurden recht detailliert beschrieben, als die Robe 1884 in Paris ausgestellt wurde (siehe Anhang II). Bezüglich dieser Robe schrieb Martin Marty: 'Ich werde sofort nach Ostern nach Rom reisen und möchte dem Heiligen Vater gern die Nachricht bringen, daß Sitting Bull der Kirche beigetreten ist. Er wird vielleicht eine Bisonrobe anfertigen, auf der der Empfang dargestellt ist, der mir im Lager am Frenchmen's Creek im Mai 1877 bereitet wurde. Ich könnte sie Leo XIII übergeben...' Obwohl belegt ist, daß es keine Bekehrung des Hunkpapa-Führers zum Katholizismus gegeben hat, erhielt Father Marty die Robe. Martys Biograph zufolge, übergab der Bischof sie persönlich im April 1885 an Leo XIII. Die Gestalten könnten jedoch den Besuch von Father Pierre-Jean De Smet im Sioux-Dorf am Powder River im Juni 1868 darstellen (siehe Abb. 1); das Treffen hier wurde mit einer umfangreichen Pfeifenzeremonie eröffnet. (Skizze von Peter Bowles.)
(Autor und Verleger danken besonders dem Künstler Peter Bowles für seine Genehmigung, die Skizze als Titelbild dieser Studie zu verwenden.)

Frontispiece: T'at'ah'ka 'Iyo'tahke (October 1881).
This rendering of "A red Napoleon" was produced by the German artist, Rudolf Cronau at Fort Randall on October 25, 1881. Cronau was much impressed by the Hunkpapa leader who was, at the time, a military prisoner. He had been sent to Fort Randall with his immediate followers after their return from Canada in July 1881. Conditions at Fort Randall were dismal and unhealthy and several prominent individuals (both red and white) campaigned for the return of the displaced Sioux to their homelands on the Grand River. This was finally accomplished in May 1883. Cronau described his initial impressions of the chief, 'a middle-sized man with a massive head, wide cheeks, prominent nose and narrow lips. His eyes covered with strange blue glasses ... dressed in a multicoloured shirt and blue leggings ... shiny black hair ... fur-wrapped plaits ... eagle feather attached to his long scalp-lock. He offered his hand ... and was glad about my visit' (Cronau 1989: 35). On departure, 'Farewell, and remember me and my people' (ibid: 39) (Translated by and with acknowledgements to, Dietmar Kuegler, Wyk).

Frontispiz: T'at'ah'ka 'Iyo'tahke (Oktober 1881).
Diese Darstellung 'Eines roten Napoleon' zeichnete der deutsche Künstler Rudolf Cronau am 25. Oktober 1881 in Fort Randall. Cronau war von dem Hunkpapa-Führer, der zu dieser Zeit Kriegsgefangener war, tief beeindruckt. Er war mit seinen engsten Anhängern nach der Rückkehr aus Kanada im Juli 1881 nach Fort Randall geschickt worden. Die Bedingungen hier waren trostlos und ungesund,

und zahlreiche prominente Personen (rote und weiße) setzten sich für eine Rückkehr der verschleppten Sioux in ihre Heimat am Grand River ein. Dazu kam es schließlich im Mai 1883. Cronau beschrieb den ersten Eindruck, den er von dem Häuptling hatte: "...eine Gestalt mittlerer Größe..., ein Mann mit einem massiven Kopfe, breiten Backenknochen, stumpfer Nase und schmalem Munde. Seine Augen wurden durch merkwürdige blaue Brillengläser verdeckt. Gekleidet ... in ein buntes Hemd und blaue Beinkleider... Glänzende schwarze Haare ... in pelzumwundene Zöpfe geflochten... In der langen Skalplocke steckte eine Adlerfeder. Er ... bot mir die Hand ... und sagte, daß er ... sich über mein Kommen freue" (Cronau, 1989: 35). Beim Abschied: "Lebe wohl und erinnere dich meiner und meines Volkes" (ibid: 39).

Figure 9 Deloria's spelling of Sitting Bull's name contrasted with the recently developed system relating to Lakota phonetics and adopted in the new Handbook of North American Indians (Vol. 17). The '$\acute{q}$' with the nasal hook used by Deloria has been retained but the raised comma in the 't' (i.e. t) has been replaced by 'h' to indicate a strong guttural sound. The nasal hooked 'a' has often been replaced by 'ah' or simply ' '. In turn the 'ah' has sometimes been rendered 'an'. These variations have caused considerable confusion in the spelling of Sitting Bull's/Supreme Bull's name. The rendering shown here, differs slightly from Deloria's original. Whose typesetter used a mirror image of the raised comma instead of a single quote. It does not matter which end of the 'apostrophe' or 'comma' has the heavy dot; what is important is the direction of the curve. The source of both marks is the Greek writing system, which used the left half of a circle for a word that begann with an 'h' sound and the right half for a word that begann with a vowel withhout the 'h'. Illustration, courtesy David Rood, Department of Linguistics. University of Colorado, Denver.

Abb. 9 Die Buchstabierung von Sitting Bulls Namen durch Deloria unterscheidet sich von dem neuerlich entwickelten System bezüglich Lakota-Phonetik, das vom neuen Handbook of North American Indians (Vol. 17) übernommen wurde. Das 'a' mit dem Nasal-Haken, das von Deloria benutzt wurde, wurde beibehalten, aber das hochgestellte Komma im 't' (d. i. t) wurde durch ein 'h' ersetzt, um einen starken gutturalen Klang anzuzeigen. Das '$\acute{q}$' mit dem Nasal-Haken wurde oft durch 'ah' oder ein einfaches 'a' ersetzt. Anderseits wurde das 'ah' manchmal als 'an' übertragen. Diese Varianten haben für erhebliche Verwirrung bei der Buchstabierung von Sitting Bulls/Supreme Bulls Namen gesorgt. Die hier vorgestellte Übertragung unterscheidet sich ein wenig von Delorias Original. Dessen Schriftsetzer benutzte ein spiegelbildliches hochgestelltes Komma, statt eines einfachen Anführungszeichens. Es ist egal, an welchem Ende des 'Apostrophs' oder 'Kommas' sich der Punkt befindet, bedeutsam ist die Ausrichtung der Krümmung. Quelle beider Markierungen ist das griechische Schriftsystem, das die linke Hälfte eines Kreises für ein Wort benutzt, dessen Anfang wie ein'H' klingt, und die rechte Hälfte für ein Wort, das mit einem Vokal ohne das 'H' beginnt. Abbildung mit Genehmigung von David Rood, Department of Linguistics. University of Colorado, Denver.

Andrew Masich • Dr. David Halaas • Dianna Litvak
Die Dog Soldiers der Cheyenne

Sie waren der bedeutendste Kriegerbund auf den Plains. Nach dem Massaker am Sand Creek, das Colorado Volunteers 1864 unter friedlichen Cheyenne anrichteten, kämpften sie als militärische Speerspitze der Plainsindianer. 1869 wurde ihr Lager bei Summit Springs von der 5. US-Kavallerie niedergemacht. 52 Dog Soldiers starben. Eine Armeekladde mit Bilderschrift - ein sogenanntes „Ledgerbook" - wurde zur Grundlage einer neuen Geschichtsschreibung über die Taten der Dog Soldiers. Für die Entschlüsselung dieser Piktographien wurden die Autoren in den USA mit dem **Choice Award** ausgezeichnet. Exklusiv für den Verlag für Amerikanistik haben sie einige ihrer wichtigsten Texte zur Geschichte der Dog Soldiers in Deutsch zusammengestellt. **Inhalt:** *Das Gefecht von Summit Springs - Das Sand Creek Massaker - Die Ledgerbook-Zeichnungen - Die Cheyenne Dog Soldiers - Die großen Kriegszüge - Die Plünderung von Julesburg - Chronologie der Geechte und Scharmützel - George Bent und das Sand Creek Massaker, u. v. m.*
64 Seiten. Großformat. 67 Abb. (12 in Farbe), Kunstdruckpapier. Geheftet.
DM 35,--

Willy Schroeter
Indianische Wohnformen
Vom Tipi zum Pueblo • Vom Wickiup zum Hogan
Vom Langhaus zur Earth Lodge

Die Wohn- u. Siedlungsformen der Völker Nordamerikas bildeten den existenziellsten Teil ihrer materiellen Kultur und zeigten mehr als andere Elemente die fundamentalen Unterschiede im indianischen Leben. Wohnung, das war Schutz und Geborgenheit, äußere Hülle für eine wohldurchdachte soziale Organisation von Familie und Gemeinschaft.

In diesem Buch hat der Hamburger Ethnologe konzentriert Bauformen und Haushaltsführung dokumentiert: Von wuchtigen Erdhütten am Oberen Missouri, über Felsklippenbauten im Südwesten, Laubhütten in den Waldländern, Iglus, Pueblos, Langhäusern, bis zu Hogans. 136 Seiten, über 90 Abb. Gebunden. **DM 39,--**

Verlag für Amerikanistik - Postf. 1332 - 25931 Wyk
Tel. 04681 / 3112 - Fax 04681 / 3258

Die größte deutsche Fachzeitschrift für indianische und amerikanische Geschichte!

MAGAZIN für Amerikanistik
Zeitschrift für amerikanische Geschichte

**Seit über 22 Jahren bewährt, kompetent, zuverlässig!
Für uns schreiben die Experten!**

In langen Planwagentrecks zogen sie nach Westen: Menschen mit dem Willen, eine neue Welt zu schaffen. Im Westen Amerikas aber erwartete sie nicht nur eine gnadenlose Natur. Es erwarteten sie auch die eigentlichen Herren des Landes, die Indianer, die ihren Besitz und ihre Kultur verteidigten und doch dem Untergang geweiht waren.
Das **MAGAZIN FÜR AMERIKANISTIK** erzählt ihre Geschichte. Die Geschichte der Indianer und der Pioniere. Seit über 22 Jahren erscheint diese populärwissenschaftliche Fachzeitschrift mit ständig wachsender Auflage. Wissenschaftler und Sachbuchautoren aus Deutschland, England, den USA und Kanada gehören zu den Mitarbeitern. Thematische Schwerpunkte sind:

- *Geschichte und Kultur der Indianer*
- *Die Besiedlung des Westens*
- *Der Amerikanische Bürgerkrieg*
- *Erscheint 4mal jährlich*
- *Format DIN A 4*
- *Umfang ca. 60 Seiten*
- *reich bebildert, teilweise farbig!*

Einige Artikel der letzten Jahrgänge:
Dr. Cath Oberholtzer: *Netzamulette der Cree*
Dietmar Kuegler: *Fort Laramie*
Helmut Petersen: *Tipibemalungen der Kiowa*
Dr. Bruno Wolters: *Heilpflanzen der Indianer*
Dr. K. A. Wipf: *Das Medizinrad*
Jens Kiecksee: *Frank Hamer, Texas Ranger*
Ron Taillon: *Bogenschießen der Hidatsa*
Michael Solka: *Louisiana Zouaves* - **Nando Stöcklin**: *Die Ojibwa* - **Dr. Joest Leopold**: *Jägerische Mythen der Jicarilla-Apachen* - **Dr. Wolfgang Hochbruck**: *Das „Turnerregiment" im Bürgerkrieg* **Andrea Blumtritt**: *Die Geistertanzbewegung und ihre Niederschlagung* - **Charles Hanson**: *James Bordeaux und der amerikanische Pelzhandel* - **D. Kuegler**: *Acoma, das Volk vom weißen Felsen* - **Tim Engelhart**: *Die Pennsylvania-Deutschen im Amerik. Bürgerkrieg* - **Klaus Listmann**: *Die Musik der Lakota* - Termine aktueller Veranstaltungen, Meldungen aus dem heutigen indianischen Amerika, Buchvorstellungen, und vieles mehr!

Abonnieren Sie diese inhaltsreiche Zeitschrift jetzt! Oder bestellen Sie **1 Probeheft** unverbindlich zum Abonnementpreis von **nur DM 7,--**.
Jahresabonnement (inkl. Versand) **nur DM 32,–** (Inland) (DM 35,– Ausland).

Verlag für Amerikanistik
Postf. 1332 - 25931 Wyk
Tel. 0 46 81 / 31 12 - Fax 0 46 81 / 32 58

Einmaliger Fachbuchkatalog mit über 90 Titeln zu den Themen
Indianer - Pionierzeit - Bürgerkrieg kostenlos!

COLIN F. TAYLOR, Ph. D., is a Senior Lecturer at Hastings College of Art and Technology, Hastings. The worldwide respected scholar published numerous books and many articles on history and culture of the Plains Indians. He holds lectures on this subject in the USA and whole Europe. In the VERLAG FÜR AMERIKANISTIK he published the following bilingual books (English & German):
Catlin's O-kee-pa - Mandan Culture and Ceremonial. The George Catlin O-kee-pa Manuscript in the British Museum
Wapa'ha, The Plains Feathered Headdress
Yupika, The Plains Indian Woman's Dress
Saam, The Symbolic Content of Early Northern Plains Ceremonial Regalia
Sun'ka Wakan, Sacred Horses of the Plains Indians
Iho'lena, Cultural, Religious and Military Content of Plains Indian Artefacts

COLIN F. TAYLOR, Dr. phil., Senior Lecturer am Hastings College of Art and Technology, Hastings. Der weltweit angesehene Wissenschaftler veröffentlichte zahlreiche Bücher und viele Artikel über Geschichte und Kultur der Plainsindianer. Er hält Vorträge über dieses Thema in den USA und ganz Europa.
Im VERLAG FÜR AMERIKANISTIK publizierte er die folgenden zweisprachigen Bücher (Deutsch & Englisch):
Catlin's O-kee-pa - Ritualismus und Zeremonialismus der Mandan. George Catlins O-kee-pa-Manuskript in den Sammlungen des British Museums
Wapa'ha, Die Plains-Federhaube
Yupika, Die Kleidung der Plainsindianer-Frauen
Saam, Der Symbolgehalt früher Zeremonialinsignien auf den nördlichen Plains
Sun'ka Wakan, Heilige Pferde der Plainsindianer
Iho'lena, Kulturelle, religiöse und militärische Inhalte von Plainsartefakten